THE CLAY SANSKRIT LIBRARY

FOUNDED BY JOHN & JENNIFER CLAY

www.claysanskritlibrary.com

www.nyupress.org

Artwork by Robert Beer.
Typeset in Adobe Garamond Pro at 10.25 : 12.3+pt.
XML-development by Stuart Brown.
Editorial input from Dániel Balogh,
Chris Gibbons, Ridi Faruque & Tomoyuki Kono.
Printed and bound in Great Britain by
T.J. International, Cornwall, on acid-free paper.

"SELF-SURRENDER" "PEACE" "COMPASSION" & "THE MISSION OF THE GOOSE"

POEMS AND PRAYERS FROM SOUTH INDIA

by APPAYYA DĪKṢITA, NĪLAKAṆṬHA DĪKṢITA & VEDĀNTA DEŚIKA

TRANSLATED BY

Yigal Bronner & David Shulman

WITH A FOREWORD BY GIEVE PATEL

NEW YORK UNIVERSITY PRESS

JJC FOUNDATION

2009

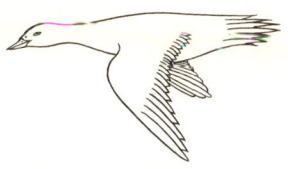

First Edition 2009

The Clay Sanskrit Library is co-published by
New York University Press
and the JJC Foundation.

Further information about this volume
and the rest of the Clay Sanskrit Library
is available at the end of this book
and on the following websites:
www.claysanskritlibrary.com
www.nyupress.org

ISBN-13: 978-0-8147-4110-8 (cloth : alk. paper)
ISBN-10: 0-8147-4110-x (cloth : alk. paper)

Library of Congress Cataloging-in-Publication Data
"Self-surrender," "Peace," "Compassion," and "The mission of the goose" :
poems and prayers from South India / by Appayya Dīkṣita, Nīlakaṇṭha Dīkṣita,
Vedānta Deśika ; translated by Yigal Bronner & David Shulman ;
with a foreword by Gieve Patel. -- 1st ed.
p. cm. -- (The Clay Sanskrit library)
Sanskrit texts with parallel English translations.
Includes bibliographical references.
ISBN-13: 978-0-8147-4110-8 (cl : alk. paper)
ISBN-10: 0-8147-4110-x (cl : alk. paper)
1. Religious poetry, Sanskrit. 2. Religious poetry, Sanskrit--
Translations into English. 3. Gods, Hindu--Poetry. 4. Hinduism--Poetry.
5. Gods, Hindu--Prayers and devotions. 6. Hinduism--Prayers and devotions.
I. Bronner, Yigal. II. Shulman, David Dean, 1949- III. Appayya Dīkṣita.
Ātmārpaṇastuti. English & Sanskrit. IV. Nīlakaṇṭha Dīkṣita, 17th cent. Śāntivilāsa.
English & Sanskrit. V. Veṅkaṭanātha, 1268-1369. Dayāśataka. English & Sanskrit.
VI. Veṅkaṭanātha, 1268-1369. Haṃsasaṃdeśa. English & Sanskrit.
PK4474.C66 2009
891'.21--dc22
2009007074

CONTENTS

CSL Conventions vii

Foreword xvii

Introduction xix

THE MISSION OF THE GOOSE

First Part 3

Prelude 5

Rama's Address to the Goose 7

The Route 15

Second Part 45

Lanka 47

The Message 67

Final Words to the Goose 77

Epilogue 79

COMPASSION 81

SELF-SURRENDER 151

PEACE 187

Notes 227

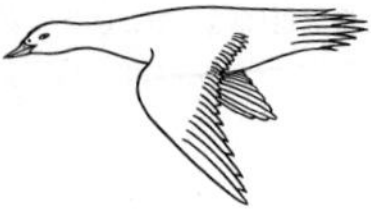

CSL CONVENTIONS

Sanskrit Alphabetical Order

Vowels:	*a ā i ī u ū ṛ ṝ ḷ ḹ e ai o au ṃ ḥ*
Gutturals:	*k kh g gh ṅ*
Palatals:	*c ch j jh ñ*
Retroflex:	*ṭ ṭh ḍ ḍh ṇ*
Dentals:	*t th d dh n*
Labials:	*p ph b bh m*
Semivowels:	*y r l v*
Spirants:	*ś ṣ s h*

Guide to Sanskrit Pronunciation

a	b*u*t
ā, â	f*a*ther
i	s*i*t
ī, î	f*ee*
u	p*u*t
ū, û	b*oo*
ṛ	vocalic *r*, American p*ur*dy or English p*re*tty
ṝ	lengthened *ṛ*
ḷ	vocalic *l*, ab*le*
e, ê, ē	m*a*de, esp. in Welsh pronunciation
ai	b*i*te
o, ô, ō	r*o*pe, esp. Welsh pronunciation; Italian s*o*lo
au	s*ou*nd
ṃ	*anusvāra* nasalizes the preceding vowel
ḥ	*visarga*, a voiceless aspiration (resembling the English *h*), or like Scottish lo*ch*, or an aspiration with a faint echoing of the last element of the preceding vowel so that *taiḥ* is pronounced *taih*[i]
k	lu*ck*
kh	blo*ckh*ead
g	*g*o
gh	bi*gh*ead
ṅ	a*n*ger
c	*ch*ill
ch	mat*chh*ead
j	*j*og
jh	aspirated *j*, he*dgeh*og
ñ	ca*ny*on
ṭ	retroflex *t*, *t*ry (with the tip of tongue turned up to touch the hard palate)
ṭh	same as the preceding but aspirated
ḍ	retroflex *d* (with the tip

	of tongue turned up to touch the hard palate)
ḍh	same as the preceding but aspirated
ṇ	retroflex *n* (with the tip of tongue turned up to touch the hard palate)
t	French *t*out
th	ten*t h*ook
d	*d*inner
dh	guil*dh*all
n	*n*ow
p	*p*ill
ph	u*ph*eaval
b	*b*efore
bh	a*bh*orrent
m	*m*ind
y	*y*es
r	trilled, resembling the Italian pronunciation of *r*
l	*l*inger
v	*w*ord
ś	*sh*ore
ṣ	retroflex *sh* (with the tip of the tongue turned up to touch the hard palate)
s	hi*ss*
h	*h*ood

CSL Punctuation of English

The acute accent on Sanskrit words when they occur outside of the Sanskrit text itself, marks stress, e.g., Ramáyana. It is not part of traditional Sanskrit orthography, transliteration, or transcription, but we supply it here to guide readers in the pronunciation of these unfamiliar words. Since no Sanskrit word is accented on the last syllable it is not necessary to accent disyllables, e.g., Rama.

The second CSL innovation designed to assist the reader in the pronunciation of lengthy unfamiliar words is to insert an unobtrusive middle dot between semantic word breaks in compound names (provided the word break does not fall on a vowel resulting from the fusion of two vowels), e.g., Maha·bhárata, but Ramáyana (not Rama·áyana). Our dot echoes the punctuating middle dot (·) found in the oldest surviving samples of written Indic, the Ashokan inscriptions of the third century BCE.

The deep layering of Sanskrit narrative has also dictated that we use quotation marks only to announce the beginning and end of every direct speech, and not at the beginning of every paragraph.

CSL Punctuation of Sanskrit

The Sanskrit text is also punctuated, in accordance with the punctuation of the English translation. In mid-verse, the punctuation will not alter the sandhi or the scansion. Proper names are capitalized. Most Sanskrit meters have four "feet" (*pāda*); where possible we print the common *śloka* meter on two lines. In the Sanskrit text, we use French *Guillemets* (e.g., *«kva saṃcicīrṣuḥ?»*) instead of English quotation marks (e.g., "Where are you off to?") to avoid confusion with the apostrophes used for vowel elision in sandhi.

SANDHI

Sanskrit presents the learner with a challenge: *sandhi* (euphonic combination). Sandhi means that when two words are joined in connected speech or writing (which in Sanskrit reflects speech), the last letter (or even letters) of the first word often changes; compare the way we pronounce "the" in "the beginning" and "the end."

In Sanskrit the first letter of the second word may also change; and if both the last letter of the first word and the first letter of the second are vowels, they may fuse. This has a parallel in English: a nasal consonant is inserted between two vowels that would otherwise coalesce: "a pear" and "an apple." Sanskrit vowel fusion may produce ambiguity.

The charts on the following pages give the full sandhi system.

Fortunately it is not necessary to know these changes in order to start reading Sanskrit. All that is important to know is the form of the second word without sandhi (pre-sandhi), so that it can be recognized or looked up in a dictionary. Therefore we are printing Sanskrit with a system of punctuation that will indicate, unambiguously, the original form of the second word, i.e., the form without sandhi. Such sandhi mostly concerns the fusion of two vowels.

In Sanskrit, vowels may be short or long and are written differently accordingly. We follow the general convention that a vowel with no mark above it is short. Other books mark a long vowel either with a bar called a macron (*ā*) or with a circumflex (*â*). Our system uses the

VOWEL SANDHI

Final vowels:

a	ā	i	ī	u	ū	ṛ	e	ai	o	au	*Initial vowels:*
' â	" â	y a	y a	v a	v a	r a	e '	ā a	o '	āv a	a
' ā	" ā	y ā	y ā	v ā	v ā	r ā	a ā	ā ā	a ā	āv ā	ā
' ê	" ê	' î	" î	v i	v i	r i	a i	ā i	a i	āv i	i
' ē	" ē	' ī	" ī	v ī	v ī	r ī	a ī	ā ī	a ī	āv ī	ī
' ô	" ô	y u	y u	' û	" û	r u	a u	ā u	a u	āv u	u
' ō	" ō	y ū	y ū	' ū	" ū	r ū	a ū	ā ū	a ū	āv ū	ū
a' r	a" r	y ṛ	y ṛ	v ṛ	v ṛ	' ṝ	a ṛ	ā ṛ	a ṛ	āv ṛ	ṛ
' âi	" âi	y e	y e	v e	v e	r e	a e	ā e	a e	āv e	e
' āi	" āi	y ai	y ai	v ai	v ai	r ai	a ai	ā ai	a ai	āv ai	ai
' âu	" âu	y o	y o	v o	v o	r o	a o	ā o	a o	āv o	o
' āu	" āu	y au	y au	v au	v au	r au	a au	ā au	a au	āv au	au

CONSONANT SANDHI

Permitted finals: k	ṭ	t	p	ṅ	n	m	*(Except āḥ/aḥ)* ḥ/r	āḥ	aḥ	*Initial letters:*
k	ṭ	t	p	ṅ	n	ṃ	ḥ	āḥ	aḥ	k/kh
g	ḍ	d	b	ṅ	n	ṃ	r	ā	o	g/gh
k	ṭ	c	p	ṅ	ṃś	ṃ	ś	āś	aś	c/ch
g	ḍ	j	b	ṅ	ñ	ṃ	r	ā	o	j/jh
k	ṭ	ṭ	p	ṅ	ṃṣ	ṃ	ṣ	āṣ	aṣ	ṭ/ṭh
g	ḍ	ḍ	b	ṅ	ṇ	ṃ	r	ā	o	ḍ/ḍh
k	ṭ	t	p	ṅ	ṃs	ṃ	s	ās	as	t/th
g	ḍ	d	b	ṅ	n	ṃ	r	ā	o	d/dh
k	ṭ	t	p	ṅ	n	ṃ	ḥ	āḥ	aḥ	p/ph
g	ḍ	d	b	ṅ	n	ṃ	r	ā	o	b/bh
ṅ	ṇ	n	m	ṅ	n	ṃ	r	ā	o	*nasals* (n/m)
g	ḍ	d	b	ṅ	n	ṃ	r	ā	o	y/v
g	ḍ	d	b	ṅ	n	ṃ	*zero*[1]	ā	o	r
g	ḍ	l	b	ṅ	l̃[2]	ṃ	r	ā	o	l
k	ṭ	c ch	p	ṅ	ñ ś/ch	ṃ	ḥ	āḥ	aḥ	ś
k	ṭ	t	p	ṅ	n	ṃ	ḥ	āḥ	aḥ	ṣ/s
gg h	ḍḍ h	dd h	bb h	ṅ	n	ṃ	r	ā	o	h
g	ḍ	d	b	ṅ/ṅṅ[3]	n/nn[3]	m	r	ā	a[4]	*vowels*
k	ṭ	t	p	ṅ	n	m	ḥ	āḥ	aḥ	*zero*

[1]ḥ or r disappears, and if a/i/u precedes, this lengthens to ā/ī/ū. [2]e.g. tān+lokān=tā̃l lokān.
[3]The doubling occurs if the preceding vowel is short. [4]Except: aḥ+a=o '.

macron, except that for initial vowels in sandhi we use a circumflex to indicate that originally the vowel was short, or the shorter of two possibilities (*e* rather than *ai*, *o* rather than *au*).

When we print initial *â*, before sandhi that vowel was *a*

î or *ê*,	*i*
û or *ô*,	*u*
âi,	*e*
âu,	*o*
ā,	*ā*
ī,	*ī*
ū,	*ū*
ē,	*ī*
ō,	*ū*
ai,	*ai*
āu,	*au*

’, before sandhi there was a vowel *a*

When a final short vowel (*a*, *i*, or *u*) has merged into a following vowel, we print ’ at the end of the word, and when a final long vowel (*ā*, *ī*, or *ū*) has merged into a following vowel we print ” at the end of the word. The vast majority of these cases will concern a final *a* or *ā*. See, for instance, the following examples:

What before sandhi was *atra asti* is represented as *atr’ âsti*

atra āste	*atr’ āste*
kanyā asti	*kany” âsti*
kanyā āste	*kany” āste*
atra iti	*atr’ êti*
kanyā iti	*kany” êti*
kanyā īpsitā	*kany” ēpsitā*

Finally, three other points concerning the initial letter of the second word:

(1) A word that before sandhi begins with *ṛ* (vowel), after sandhi begins with *r* followed by a consonant: *yatha” rtu* represents pre-sandhi *yathā ṛtu*.

(2) When before sandhi the previous word ends in *t* and the following word begins with *ś*, after sandhi the last letter of the previous word is *c*

and the following word begins with *ch*: *syāc chāstravit* represents pre-sandhi *syāt śāstravit*.

(3) Where a word begins with *h* and the previous word ends with a double consonant, this is our simplified spelling to show the pre-sandhi form: *tad hasati* is commonly written as *tad dhasati*, but we write *tadd hasati* so that the original initial letter is obvious.

COMPOUNDS

We also punctuate the division of compounds (*samāsa*), simply by inserting a thin vertical line between words. There are words where the decision whether to regard them as compounds is arbitrary. Our principle has been to try to guide readers to the correct dictionary entries.

Exemplar of CSL Style

Where the Devanagari script reads:

कुम्भस्थली रक्षतु वो विकीर्णसिन्धूररेणुर्द्विरदाननस्य ।
प्रशान्तये विघ्नतमश्छटानां निष्ठ्यूतबालातपपल्लवेव ॥

Others would print:

kumbhasthalī rakṣatu vo vikīrṇasindūrareṇur dviradānanasya /
praśāntaye vighnatamaśchaṭānāṃ niṣṭhyūtabālātapapallaveva //

We print:

kumbha|sthalī rakṣatu vo vikīrṇa|sindūra|reṇur dvirad'|ānanasya
praśāntaye vighna|tamaś|chaṭānāṃ niṣṭhyūta|bāl'|ātapa|pallav" êva.

And in English:

May Ganésha's domed forehead protect you! Streaked with vermilion dust, it seems to be emitting the spreading rays of the rising sun to pacify the teeming darkness of obstructions.

("Nava·sáhasanka and the Serpent Princess" 1.3)

Wordplay

Classical Sanskrit literature can abound in puns (*śleṣa*). Such paronomasia, or wordplay, is raised to a high art; rarely is it a *cliché*. Multiple meanings merge (*śliṣyanti*) into a single word or phrase. Most common are pairs of meanings, but as many as ten separate meanings are attested. To mark the parallel senses in the English, as well as the punning original in the Sanskrit, we use a *slanted* font (different from *italic*) and a triple colon (⁝) to separate the alternatives. E.g.

yuktaṃ Kādambarīṃ śrutvā kavayo maunam āśritāḥ
Bāṇa|dhvanāv an|adhyāyo bhavat' îti smṛtir yataḥ.

It is right that poets should fall silent upon hearing the Kádambari, for the sacred law rules that recitation must be suspended when *the sound of an arrow ⁝ the poetry of Bana* is heard.

(Soméshvara·deva's "Moonlight of Glory" I.15)

For Eileen and Galila.

dahr juz jalva-i yaktāy-i ma'shūq nahīṃ.
ham kahāṃ hote agar ḥusn na hotā khod-bīn?

Time doesn't exist
but for the moment I remove the veil
from my only love.
Can *we* exist
if beauty won't see
itself?

—Ghaleb

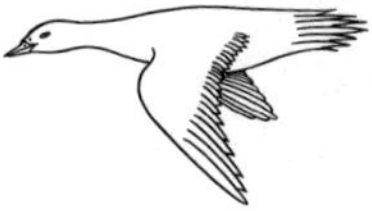

FOREWORD

A contemporary poet tends to visit the poetry of the past in the spirit of a hunter. Sure he will be full of awe and respect where these are due, but the wish to cannibalize will be paramount. Where it comes to poetry written in a language other than the one this poet habitually uses, such cannibalizing is not possible in the absence of a superb translation: an entirely fresh creation written in the language this poet uses, but built on the bones of the earlier poetry.

I have read the post-medieval Sanskrit poetry in this volume, all the while harboring such dubious hunger. SHULMAN and BRONNER's translations are magnificent. The poetry leaps across a millennium, speaks directly to my modern consciousness. The one possible obstacle, my inability to fully participate in a Vaishnavite or Shaivite belief system, is overcome by the universality of the human situations that are evoked and elaborated.

I can think of two successful attempts at incorporating earlier poetry in modern works: ARUN KOLATKAR and A.K. RAMANUJAN. As it happens both were very accomplished translators of earlier poetry. In the case of RAMANUJAN, "Fear No Fall," a poem on the South Indian poet-saint Arunagiri published posthumously after RAMANUJAN's untimely death in 1993, gives us an inkling of the kinds of terrain he would have investigated had he lived longer.

Will SHULMAN and BRONNER's translations catalyze a possible creative awakening in the sacred/secular area that these post-medieval poems explore? The works in this volume are auspicious in their range and scope. And the wonderful introduction, both scholarly and lucid, gives us ample help where our understanding might falter.

These great Sanskrit poems in the translations given them here will be read and re-read by lovers of poetry over the years. Fresh insights await the reader at every turn. I would like to end my foreword by pointing out just one of the many felicities that are special to these verses: the quality of reiteration. This reiteration is not incantatory. Nor is it in the nature of variations on a theme. Rather, each succeeding verse is a re-assertion through a fresh experience, so that experience is piled upon experience, a heaping of richness upon richness that leaves you with a sense of the unending fecundity of the imagination. The verses rush out at you from an invisible, unlocatable source, seemingly an inexhaustible one.

GIEVE PATEL
Mumbai, February 2009

INTRODUCTION

THIS VOLUME seeks to explore the expressive possibilities of Sanskrit in late medieval and premodern South India, a period of intense interaction among different literary languages and cultural formations. We present four works, strongly and intricately interlinked, that could be broadly classed as prayer or devotional lyric. All are well-known compositions by prominent poet-intellectuals from the Tamil country, although they fall outside of the conventional canon of classical Sanskrit works as taught in modern academic settings. In their own time, these works traveled widely in the south and spoke to a large audience of cultivated and engaged readers or listeners of various backgrounds and persuasion. We also feel that each, in its own right, is a gem of Sanskrit poetry.

The second millennium CE, as SHELDON POLLOCK (2006: 283ff.) has demonstrated, saw the rise and self-assertion of India's vernaculars as literary languages. Yet rather than fade away, or "die," the cosmopolitan idiom of Sanskrit became an important player in a new linguistic economy and in the creation of regional literary visions.[1] Sanskrit writers of the second millennium utilized the unique intertextual and interlinguistic resources available to poets who were both immersed in the tradition and part of a lively vernacular environment in order to achieve expressive depths perhaps not possible before. Elsewhere, we have even formulated a principle, or a hypothesis: as localization increases, what is lost in geographical range is made up for by increasing complexity and depth (BRONNER & SHULMAN 2006). We will attempt to illustrate and substantiate this hypothesis in the following pages, particularly but not solely, in reference to the first work we discuss, Vedánta Déshika's "Mission of the Goose" (*Haṃsasandeśa*).

Vedánta Déshika: Philosopher-Poet

Vedánta Déshika, or more precisely Vénkata·natha (1268–1369), is usually classed as a theologian, indeed perhaps, after Ramánuja, the most intellectually powerful and influential of the teachers (*ācāryas*) of the South Indian religion of Vishnu worship. He is, moreover, the dominant voice in the so-called northern branch (*vaḍakalai*) of South Indian Shri Vaishnavism, which differs from the southern branch (*tenkalai*) on a series of critical theological points. Perhaps the most prominent of these is the question of agency: northerners stress the human agent's autonomous effort in winning God's attention and mercy, whereas the southern school asserts that god's mercy acts unconditionally, regardless of human activity. This difference is typically captured by contrasting images of the devotee as either a baby monkey or a kitten. The monkey actively holds on to its mother, while the kitten is passively carried—the mother holds the kitten by the neck in her teeth. These two analogies—the monkey paradigm (*markaṭa/kiśora/nyāya*) and the kitten paradigm (*mārjāra/kiśora/nyāya*)—serve as emblems of the contrastive theology and anthropology of the schools and also turn up in artistic and literary texts. In addition, the southern school enhances the role of the feminine persona of God generally, with many far-reaching implications, while the northern tends to a more male-oriented view of Vishnu. Another difference is a pronounced preference among the southerners for Tamil, rather than Sanskrit, as the medium for both poetic and religious expression.

Friedhelm Hardy (1979) has shown in a highly nuanced analysis of another poem by Vedánta Déshika, the "Song of the Threshold" (*Dehalīśastuti*), that this champion of the northerners has strong secret affinities with the southern school; we will develop this point further. Hardy also pointed to Vedánta Déshika's dual persona as poet as well as philosopher, as we see in one of his recurrent epithets *kavi/tārkika/siṃha*, a lion among poets and logicians. We might take these observations further and argue that the severely normative image of this great figure as first and foremost an orthodox Tamil Brahmin obscures his identity as one of the boldest and most imaginative poets in the entire history of the Sanskrit literary tradition. We think of him as a radical innovator, one of the first to combine in profound and complex ways not only the competing theologies of the Shri Vaishnava subsects but also, and more consequentially, the different sensibilities of Sanskrit and Tamil poetry. The texts we have chosen to translate, while very different in nature, exemplify this innovative moment; though it is important to bear in mind that Vedánta Déshika left behind a vast literary corpus in Sanskrit, Tamil, and Prakrit that includes many remarkable hymns of praise (*stotras*), a major narrative poem on the life of Krishna, the "Deeds of Krishna" (*Yādavābhyudaya*), as well as a long allegorical play, the "Sunrise of Resolution" (*Saṅkalpasūryodaya*).[2]

The "Mission of the Goose" (*Haṃsasandeśa*) belongs to the highly productive genre of "messenger-poems," modeled after Kali·dasa's classic, the "Cloud Messenger" (*Megha-sandeśa*, also known as the *Meghadūta*).[3] Formally, these are love poems, structured around a message sent by an exiled lover to his faraway beloved, often via a surprising carrier: a cloud, the wind, a variety of birds, bees, and so on. In general, both the message and the detailed map given to the courier are highly imaginative enterprises. Most of these messenger poems share many formal features and a virtually identical structure: a five-verse introductory apostrophe to the chosen messenger culminating in an explicit acknowledgement of the bizarre nature of the entire mission; then a preliminary description of the projected route, followed by a detailed and longer portrayal of selected individual sites along the way; eventually the messenger is imagined as arriving at his destination—marking a transition to the second section of the work—where he is gradually guided to the beloved, who is lovingly described; he introduces himself to her and delivers the poetic message, which includes a promise of reunion.[4] All of this harks back to Kali·dasa's prototype, which has also fixed the elegant and melodic *mandākrāntā* meter[5] as obligatory for subsequent works in the genre. This format is reproduced to the letter by Vedánta Déshika, who thus superimposes a cosmopolitan Sanskrit template on the geographical, social, and religious world of Tamil poetry.

By way of contrast, the "Century on Compassion" (*Dayā-śataka*) is a Sanskrit poem written in the format of Tamil devotional hymns. Like them, it consists of ten decades (*patikam*s), each with its own thematic consistency and separate meter, plus a short epilogue of a metapoetic and biographical nature. Typically, such devotional works, many of them incorporated in the Tamil canons of poems to Shiva and Vishnu, posit an intimate relationship between the poet-devotee and a divinity localized at a particular South Indian shrine. In the present case, Vedánta Déshika imagines the abstract aspect of God's compassion as a local goddess, living at the mountain temple of Tirupati, on the northern border of the Tamil-speaking region. This mountain is home to lord Venkatéshvara, a form of Vishnu, and to his official wives, the celestial Lakshmi, Bhu·devi or Earth, and the dark Nila (as well as today, at least, his local bride Padmávati or Alarmel·mangai). Thus here, too, but in a very different manner, Sanskrit is used to express highly local and regional concerns and sensibilities and to create a cultural space, with its own aesthetics and theology.

"The Mission of the Goose": The Depths of Space and Time

"The Mission of the Goose" (*Haṃsasandeśa*) is a complex lyrical interlude inserted, as it were, into a critical juncture of the "Ramáyana." After a long and frustrating search, Rama has finally received a first sign of life from his beloved wife Sita, who has been kidnapped by the demon Rávana and held captive ever since. Rama's new ally, the monkey Hánuman, has just returned from Lanka, which he reached by leaping over a vast stretch of the ocean, and where he managed to find Sita and speak with her. After debriefing Hánuman, Rama has made arrangements to set off immediately, with his army of monkeys, for Lanka. In Vedánta Déshika's poem, Rama, sleepless with longing and impatient to communicate with Sita, happens upon a goose and entrusts it with an urgent message to his wife.

"The Mission of the Goose" is aimed at an audience that is intimately familiar with Kali·dasa's prototype of the messenger poem. This is not only a matter of formal or structural replication, or even the occasional verbatim repetition of phrases from Kali·dasa's work. Rather, the relationship between the two poems is an explicit and recurrent theme in the "Mission of the Goose." Clouds have a particular salience throughout the poem, always to ironic or even subversive effects. Look, for example, at the following verse from the "Cloud Messenger" and its precise reflection in exactly the same slot in the "Mission of the Goose":

Smoke, light, water and wind put together:
what does a cloud have to do with such a serious matter?
Doesn't it take a person, fully awake, to deliver a message?
But the yaksha *didn't think it through when he made*
his request.
Lovers, if they're miserable enough, can't tell
the living from the still. ("Cloud Messenger" 1.5)[6]

A goose knows nothing of messages, yet
Rama approached him with great respect.
(Not even Hánuman received such honor.)
In his utter madness he found a way
into the bird's heart. People shaken by separation
are reduced to begging help from clouds,
mountains, trees, and so on—to say nothing
of living creatures. ("The Mission of the Goose" 1.5)

We have the same question, the same logical structure, the same rhetorical device of resorting to a generalization about human nature (*arth'|ântara|nyāsa*); some of the vocabulary is shared; even the verse number is the same. And yet there is a subtle difference in tone. For all the pathos, Vedánta Déshika's verse also makes us smile. We happen to know of a case where someone asked even a cloud to be his messenger. In fact, as will become clear later on, this obvious reference to the famous intertext also includes a slight "dig." Rama's choice of messenger, we are told, actually makes better sense. And in the course of noticing this similarity and this difference, including the irony that accompanies the intertextual conversation, one begins to sense the opening up of a certain unfamiliar, promising space.

The irony soon deepens. Clouds keep turning up in pointed reference. For example:

In the absence of a noble songbird,
these bird-brained peacocks never shut up.
They go mad. It happened
in the rains, when you took off for Kailása.
But clouds are history.
As you make your way south,
you'll have the utter pleasure
of seeing these peacocks, shorn of their feathers,
gone silent. ("The Mission of the Goose" 1.10)

Sanskrit peacocks screech and dance in ecstasy as soon as they catch sight of the monsoon clouds. This verse seemingly celebrates the relief one gets when the rains subside and the peacocks stop their annoying clamor. However, there is another, highly conspicuous linguistic register operating in the verse. *Sat/kavi*, "noble bird" normally means "a good poet"—so, in the absence of such a poet, the "bird-brain peacocks" (*jaḍa/dhiyām.... vipina/śikhinām*) will here mean "boorish brahmins," who have a field day, chattering idiocies that deafen the ears. They only quiet down when the clouds—or the Cloud—retreat and the true poet returns. Suddenly they are shorn of their phony feathers, and the real poet can enjoy their naked silence.

We are, in effect, in a sequel to the "Cloud Messenger"; the season has changed from monsoon to autumn, and the goose is now headed back south after his north-bound flight during the rains. On top of this change we have a rather direct attack on a whole crowd of poetasters, a common topos in *kāvya*. However, the most striking feature of this verse is the strategically placed phrase *megh'/âpāye*, literally "at the departure of the cloud," which quite explicitly names the significant intertext and at the same time sets it aside. Kali·dasa and his cloud are history. So are the chatterbox poets who followed in Kali·dasa's path, like the peacocks that welcome the cloud messenger in his *Meghasandeśa*.[7] It is as if Vedánta Déshika were telling us that the *Meghasandeśa* had to be superseded so that his own composition could emerge in all its uniqueness. The "Cloud" is gone, although its absence remains as a constant presence.

But the *Meghasandeśa* is by no means the only intertext evoked in the *Haṃsasandeśa*. Consider, for example, the following verse from a different work by Kali·dasa, the "Lineage of the Raghus" (*Raghuvaṃśa* 13.23):

This is the place.
I was searching for you and I found,
thrown on the ground, one anklet
wrapped in silence, as if in grief
at being torn from your foot,
soft as a lotus.[8]

Rama and Sita are finally together, flying back from Lanka to their capital of Ayódhya in the aerial chariot put at their disposal by the new demon king Vibhíshana (now that Rávana has been slain). While in the air, they retrace the trajectory of their wanderings in reverse, re-experiencing both the traumas and the joys of their years in the wilderness. They are now passing over the area where, shortly after the kidnapping, Sita cast down some personal items in the hope that Rama would find them and trace her: among them was a single anklet, one of a pair. Kali·dasa's limpid, musical verse, with its imaginative attribution of a conscious reason for the anklet's silence (the figure is called *het'|ûtprekṣā*), powerfully suggests the intense loneliness of the separated lover, recalled with a certain nostalgia, now that the pair has been reunited.

Now look at *Haṃsasandeśa* 2.20, where Rama is describing to the goose his projected image of Sita (this is a part of a long sequence of verses meant to prepare the goose for its emotional meeting with Sita):

And this right anklet of hers—
the one that rings like your voice—
walked away from her foot
and came down to earth as if to show me

the way. Its twin—the one that I
should be tying to her lotus foot
when it comes to rest on my lap—
is hidden high in a branch above her.
I'm sure that whenever she looks at it,
her heart sinks.

Follow the movement. We now have two eloquent messengers—the goose, whose call recalls the tinkling of Sita's anklets, and the right anklet itself, clearly the same one we met, wrapped in silence, in the *Raghuvaṃśa* verse. These messengers fly off in opposite directions. The anklet "walked away" towards Rama; the goose will shortly be taking off in the opposite, southerly direction. We also have two anklets—the right one, which Rama holds in his hand, and the left one that is secretly kept by Sita, hidden on a branch of the *śiṃśapā* tree in Lanka under which she is kept captive. Rama looks down at "his" anklet; Sita looks up at hers. Moreover, each anklet belongs to a different temporal direction. The right one points backwards in time to the moment of kidnapping; the left one embodies the future moment of intimate reunion, when Rama will tie it to Sita's foot.[9] Taken together, we have in concrete form both separation and union, despair and hope.

It is as if Vedánta Déshika has deliberately engaged with this specific verse from the *Raghuvaṃśa*, with its meditation on the symbology of the lonely anklet and its psychology of separation. This same anklet now bears a much heavier expressive burden. For one thing, it is no longer silent; it is yet another eloquent messenger. For another, it is a far more complex token in a temporal and semiotic sense. The *Raghuvaṃśa* anklet is part of the essentially linear play of memory: the whole emphasis is on recalling the agony of loss, which is beyond language. But for Vedánta Déshika's Rama, the moment of loss, just like its token, is twinned with its opposite. Two conflicting temporal vectors are conflated, as if they were unrolling simultaneously, just as the two lovers, in their respective spatial settings, are united in a simultaneous, contrasting imagining of each other—through the two mirroring and displaced anklets. The reader, especially if he or she knows the intertext, experiences a dizzying density as the verse unfolds. Such density, we believe, is the hallmark of the "Mission of the Goose" as a whole.

It is enough here to focus briefly on three aspects of this density, already hinted in the above verse: density of space, time, and divine presence.[10] Perhaps the most readily apparent of these aspects is the thematization of South Indian space, or rather the Tamil country, as highly saturated matter. The poet even has a term for this densely compacted geography—*saṃhati*, as we can see in the following verse, where Rama outlines the routes available for the goose:

Hánuman has ably mapped out for me
two alternative routes. One takes you west
over the Sahya Hills. Though shorter,
it's not particularly pleasant, due to incessant rain.
The problem with the east is its endless attractions
that in place after place will dazzle your eyes.
But for my sake, friend,
you'll just have to look away.
("The Mission of the Goose" 1.18)

"Endless attractions" is our translation for *saṃhatāv adbhūtānām*, literally, a dense mass of wonders. The western route, that is Kerala, apparently lacks the concentration of interesting and diverting sites with which the Tamil country, in the east, is blessed. This eastern trajectory is dangerously fascinating, and Rama has to beg the goose not to lose too much time enjoying its numerous attractions. Needless to say, his supplication has, for the poem's readers or listeners, the opposite effect of Rama's intention; the subsequent verses will linger over these very attractions, thereby fully mapping the imagined cultural space that will displace Kali·dasa's poetic geography. The flight of the goose weaves together elements belonging to distinct registers of regional identity—the major polities that came to be seen as constituting the Tamil political order (Pállavas/Tundíras, Cholas and Pandyas); the conventionalized landscapes (*tiṇai*) of old Tamil poetry (thus the mountain region of Tirupati fits the ancient *kuriñci* landscape; the Kallar land is a direct transposition of the *pālai* wilderness; the Chola delta is the prototypical *marutam* zone; and the exquisite description of the southern coast is *neytal*); an idealized social spectrum including peasant women, pearl-fishers, thieves, yogis, warriors and gods; the great Vaishnava temples beginning, appropriately, with Tirupati and moving through the Várada·raja shrine at Kanchi·puram (Hasti·giri) and Shri·rangam to Alagar·malai outside Madurai. All this is plotted on the grid of major rivers, mountains and cities.

What makes this Tamil space so dense is its repeated incorporation of a powerful vertical dimension: virtually every point on the visible surface is opened up to presences descending from above or ascending from below. At Tirupati, for example, "human beings climb up this mountain/ and gods climb down to it from heaven," so that "high and low disappear" (1.22). White Cliff, further south and west, is compared to "a sliver of silver Kailása," the great mountain of the north, as if "sinking into the ground," but also to "the giant snake from the netherworld, stretching his brilliant hood" (1.38). Even water is not the innocent liquid you might think. In fact, at Shri·rangam, water from all over the world has come on pilgrimage to the Chandra·púshkarini pond and apparently stayed on there in condensed form. The moon, too, came down for a dip to cure himself from a disease (the treatment worked). That same pond, the goose is promised, will quench his craving for Mánasa Lake—his nesting place in the Himalayas and an important stop on the cloud's route in Kali·dasa's intertext (1.44). Indeed, we can see here a general pattern recurring throughout the "Mission of the Goose": the Tamil country, especially in its temple sites, regularly surpasses the celestial and the divine, so that it becomes, as the poet tells us, "a heaven on earth" (1.31). No wonder that the goose, flying over this marvelous route, "will pine no more for Paradise" (1.40). This unique privileging of the southern world *vis-à-vis* all other cosmic spheres reaches its climax in the second half of the poem, with the description of Lanka, replete with imprisoned goddesses, heavenly chariots, wishing trees from heaven, and above all, the presence of Sita herself.

Temporality shows a similarly complex compacting. In fact, one might go so far as to claim that the poem as a whole is a meditation on the differential aspects and experiences of time. The very first verse tells us that, following Hánuman's return, Rama could barely get through the night "that seemed to stretch on forever until dawn" (1.1). This stretching out of time is one of several temporal possibilities. Time may be experienced as broken into fragments (2.33), frozen still (1.1), as hurrying forward with the urgent mission of uniting the lovers (2.41), or as moving simultaneously in different directions and thus infinitely condensed. Thus one of the startling features of life in Lanka is the fact that "all six seasons work round the clock" (2.7).

On some surface level, the separated lovers suffer from a sense that time, which once raced by when they were together, has now painfully slowed down, even broken down as a natural force. This notion comes through forcefully when Rama speaks directly to Sita, in the very first verse of his imaginary message, and depicts the unbearable gap between the nights of the past, which "passed like a second," and that of the present which, "shattered / into pieces by countless images of loving / and too many thoughts, never ends" (2.33). Often, however, these very different modes seem to operate simultaneously. Here is how Rama imagines Sita's daily routine:

... Maybe she's cross-examining the birds for news
of my arrival, or scanning the horizon, her eyes veiled
by tears, for signs that some word from her lover
is imminent. She might even be conversing
with her ornaments, hidden somewhere nearby: "Do you
or do you not remember what it feels like to be touched
by Rama?" Or she could be absorbed in the joys
of lying together, in a single bed, though they are now

long past. Fate has reduced her, I'm sure, to these ways of killing time. ("The Mission of the Goose" 1.11–12)

On the one hand, Sita is desperately trying to pass the time (*kāla/yātrā*), even to kill it, like every prisoner. On the other hand, she is apparently capable of entering a meditative trance (*dhyāyantī*), in which Rama is again beside her, in the same bed. And although these joys are now long past, we readers know that they also lie in the future. Indeed, the future is already present in the verse, in several diverse forms—in the message that Rama knows Sita is waiting for, and which he is now proleptically reciting to the goose; in Sita's anxious gaze at the horizon; and in her apostrophe to her ornaments, reminiscent of the two temporal modes embodied by her anklets in verse 2.20 discussed above. Perhaps most striking of all, however, is the synchronicity of action and feeling: both lovers are experiencing the same bizarrely concurrent temporal rhythms, infused with memory, impatience, and a clear vision of the future. Both, too, seem to be spending a lot of time talking to birds. In a sense, this perfect symmetry already makes the future present. The present moment, painful as it may be, is thus saturated with both past and future.

An important theological point lurks here. After all, Kali·dasa's "Cloud Messenger," another insistent voice from the past, has already set up these parameters of symmetrical longing as signs of the projected reunion. Vedánta Déshika's text, however, takes a significant further step by positing and demonstrating that the reality of togetherness, in this case togetherness with God, necessarily pervades and indeed overpowers the experience of separation. This realization finds its ultimate expression in verse 2.40, perhaps the most beautiful of the entire poem, clearly meant to be paired with Kali·dasa's famous "Cloud Messenger" 2.42. For the sake of comparison, we first translate Kali·dasa's verse:

Body into body,
the lean to the lean,
fierce fire into fire,
tears into flowing tears,
longing into ceaseless longing,
heavy sigh to endless sigh:
he who is far
enters you
in his thoughts,
while hostile fate blocks his path.[11]

Now Vedánta Déshika's creative equivalent to this powerful poem:

Our bodies touch
in the southern wind.
Our eyes meet
in the moon.
We live together in a single home—
the world, and the earth
is the one bed we share.
The sky scattered with stars
is a canopy stretched above us.
Think of this, my lean beauty:
However far away
fate has taken you from me,

I still find my way
into you.

The echoes are persistent, as we expect them to be. Where Kali·dasa begins with the body (*aṅga*), Vedánta Déshika begins with a synonym, *deha*. The intense interweaving of the Kali·dasa verse is clearly also the theme in Vedánta Déshika's. Both verses end with a complaint against fate, *vidhi*, which is responsible for the distance separating the lovers (*dūravartī*, *dūrībhūtā*). Yet the contrast is no less striking. Look, for example, at the word order of the final line: Kali·dasa moves from the imagined fusion embodied in the verb *viśati*, "enters," to the harsh reality of blockage (*ruddha / mārgaḥ*). Vedánta Déshika builds up, in a fantastic crescendo, to the final verb *nirviśāmi*, "I enter," "delight in," "make love to." On the way up we have the juxtaposed pronouns inseparably conjoined: *tvām aham*, "I-you." Remember that this is God speaking to his beloved, with whom he does, truly, share a single universe, despite the undeniable experience of distance.

Both poems envisage the lovers' union—but how different it is! For Kali·dasa, the togetherness can come about only in the imagination (*saṃkalpaiḥ*), which stands to be frustrated or contradicted by reality. But in the "Mission of the Goose," with its concrete reference to all the components of a physical world, the union is factual and real. Moreover, the very simplicity of reference—to the wind, the moon, the earth, the stars—both domesticates and endears. We, the listeners, also experience a magical intimacy with the divine. We, too, live in his home and sleep in his bed.

And there is a further complication. On top of all other temporal planes we repeatedly hear the poet speaking out of his own present moment, which is far in the future relative to story of his characters. After all, the landscape as described to the goose, with cities, shrines, and pilgrimage centers, is the Tamil country as it was known to Vedánta Déshika. Perhaps the most telling example of this added temporal complexity of perceptual depth is found in the description of the main shrine at Shri·rangam, one of the two main temples of Southern Shri Vaishnavism and at one point the home of our poet:

It was installed on the bank of this lake.
It is worshiped by good people.
Make sure you go there too,
my friend,
and bow in good faith
to the Shesha Throne.
For, as the sages have predicted,
Shri Ranga·natha—now stationed in Ayódhya,
fortunately for my family—
will make his home there
one day. ("The Mission of the Goose" 1.45)

The verse starts off with the simple, linear progression through time of the Shesha Throne, on which the god of Shri·rangam reclines. It was once installed beside the temple lake. It is currently being worshipped by *sādhu*s, or good people. The goose would do well to pay it a visit on his route. All this is reported from the poetic present, i.e., Rama's perspective as he sends the goose off to Lanka. Note that at this poetic moment, the Shesha Throne is not yet occupied. This absence stands in stark contrast to the poet's present in which the sanctuary is entirely active and perfectly in place. Indeed, Vedánta Déshika, like everyone in his intended audience, knows very well how this important structure came to be there: originally a mobile shrine located in Ayódhya, it was given by Rama to Vibhíshana as a gift in return for his help and loyalty in the Lanka war. Vibhíshana tried to take it home to Lanka, but on the way he put it down in Shri·rangam in order to celebrate a festival with the Chola king. When he tried to pick it up, he could not move it; the god appeared and informed him that the shrine would remain permanently at Shri·rangam as a result of austerities performed by the Kavéri River, and that he himself intended to stay there, too.[12] The only problem is that this entire prior history of the shrine still lies in Rama's future. Rama has yet to meet Vibhíshana, so the Shesha Throne should, in theory, be empty. Indeed, the mobile shrine is still parked in Ayódhya, with the god's image inside it.

On the other hand, the goose has no reason to visit the Shri·rangam temple if it is not the home of Shri Ranga·natha. So the two presents, with their separate needs and realities, conflict. A solution is found by positing Rama's prior knowledge, based on what the sages have predicted, of the future to be enacted at this site. This makes the goose a time-traveler who is, in effect, visiting the future. Moreover, he is about to visit the very person who is sending him off—for Rama is contemplating the future of another aspect of himself, an aspect he apparently values and even worships. He is directing the goose to perform a prophetic act of *pūjā* to his currently unoccupied throne—to bow to someone who is not yet there. We might say that Rama is sending regards to other parts of himself that will come into existence in a future time that we, the listeners or readers, already inhabit. In this sense, we too are living in the future.

Note that the goose is moving in at least two temporal vectors at once. The poet has, as it were, sent him backwards into the past, while the hero of the poem propels him into the future. "Goose-time" apparently is capable of such loops. Think again of the relative temporality of this messenger poem *vis-à-vis* its model. It takes place both before and after Kali·dasa's "Cloud Messenger." On the one hand, the "Ramáyana" lies in the mythic memory of the hero-lover of the "Cloud Messenger" who, at one point, even compares his messenger, the cloud, to Rama's original messenger, Hánuman.[13] Thus the "Mission of the Goose" throws us back in time to a point before the cloud's mission—indeed, to that point in time when Hánuman's mission has just taken place. On the other hand, the "Mission of the Goose" is clearly a sequel to the "Cloud Messenger" and structures itself on all levels accordingly. Moreover, it takes place, as the poet repeatedly tells us, when clouds have become "history."

It would be possible to extend this discussion still further and to reveal additional temporal nuances at work in the poem's verses. The reader is invited to try to work them out with his or her own intuitions. But one thing, at least, should be clear. A poetic world replete with such richly crisscrossing temporal, spatial, and theological dimensions is a world of astonishing depth. In part this depth reflects the interweaving of several literary corpora—classical Sanskrit poetry (such as the works of Kali·dasa mentioned above), the great Sanskrit epics (in this case the "Ramáyana"), and local traditions in both the vernacular and the Sanskrit (e.g. "The Greatness of Shri·rangam" (*Śrīraṅga-māhātmya*) and the canonical Tamil poems of the Shri Vaishnava devotees, or *Āḻvār*s). These three sets of intertexts create a continuous resonance that can only be found in Sanskrit poetry of the second millennium. This is not to say that all the Sanskrit works of this period measure up to Vedánta Déshika's standards. We are clearly dealing with a poet of genius.

We can sketch in the contours of what "genius" might mean in this context. Apart from the sheer linguistic and musical virtuosity, evident throughout his oeuvre, Vedánta Déshika constantly displays in this work a complex and sometimes ironic awareness of his unique place within a millennium-old tradition. Above we began to chart the intertextual richness that is built in to the very structure of the "Cloud Messenger." The main point, however, is not the mere presence of a set of intertexts, but their radical and conscious reconfiguration and the expressive power that it enables. This is the work of a poet of amazing self-confidence and audacity. Along with this bold self-awareness comes a mordant sense of humor and an ironic tone aimed at his subject matter (consider, in particular, his consistent and somewhat sarcastic depictions of Rávana's well-appointed capital and palace) and at his own poetic forefathers. On the other hand, what we do not find in Vedánta

Déshika is a strong sense of self-irony or self-deprecation, such as we shall see, for example, in Nila·kantha Díkshita. Rather, Vedánta Déshika sees himself, somewhat like his chosen heroine, Sita, as operating in a grimly hostile and philistine environment. For Sita, in her captivity, is not only "a burst of pure moonlight in the dog-eater's hut," but also "a lyrical line by a real poet sung to a mean-hearted crowd." (2.13).

"Compassion": The Iron Shackles of Mercy

"Compassion" (*Dayāśataka*) is driven by a passionate re-imagining of the Shri Vaishnava deity and the dynamics of his relations to human beings. Ostensibly, this male god lives securely in his temple home on the top of Vénkatam Hill, consistently referred to as Bull Hill in this poem. From there, he keeps watch, as it were, on the workings of the cosmos he created, the ups and downs of karmic causality, and the consequent business of judging all of us for our various deeds and misdeeds. In fact, however, this rational and male-dominated conceptual system is radically subverted by that aspect of God that the poet calls Compassion (*dayā*, *karuṇā*, *anukampā*), visualized as an autonomous female force within him. Indeed, the entire mountain, home to this god, is nothing but a crystallized form of this gushing flood of mercy, as the poet tells us in the very first verse. Thus pilgrims who climb the mountain to see the deity are actually walking on or in Compassion embodied. Moreover, everything that takes place on this mountain, including the crucial interplay between God, devotee, and herself, is entirely masterminded by Compassion: she is the reason that Vishnu came to this mountain in the first place, as she is the source of all of his manifestations in the world (see, e.g., 28, 81–90), and she is the real reason that pilgrims come to Bull Hill to seek him.

The English word "compassion" cannot convey the full intensity and velocity of Daya as Vedánta Déshika conceives of her. What really fascinates the poet is the profound wildness of this aspect of God. She is totally free from any constraints or calculations and beyond any rule or logic, though she is occasionally fond of giving us the illusion that her merciful actions are part of some meaningful scheme (see, e.g., 74). The truth is that she eludes all such considerations: she enacts the reality of total freedom and insists on forcing it on us (e.g. 75–76). This propensity is depicted throughout the poem as irrational, even crazy, something that astonishes the whole world including God himself:

What a crazy idea! What's going on?
The whole world smiles in disbelief
and the God on Lion Hill gasps
in admiration when you, Compassion,
stand waiting at the crossroads
of Veda City, to welcome
anyone who turns up in the tattered cloak
of surrender, with nothing to offer
but misdeeds. ("Compassion" 70)

Surrender here refers to the Shri Vaishnava goal of *prapatti* or *śaraṇāgati*, that is, the devotee's complete offering of his or her self to God. As mentioned above, the northern school regards this critical act as a voluntary, active decision on the part of the devotee. In a certain sense this vision comes through in the verse just cited, since the new arrivals at Veda City have indeed made the journey with the intention of literally surrendering their burden at the Lord's feet. However, this supreme act is no more than a tattered disguise. What really matters is the headlong rush of Compassion to welcome these pathetic beggars on the road. Moreover, as the southern school might have posited, Compassion is acting independently, out of her own inner necessity and nature, regardless of the devotees' own intentionality. In fact, she often behaves in ways that are completely contrary to their thoughts, inclinations and objectives, let alone their acts:

> *There are those who live near Bull Hill*
> *for all the wrong reasons, their lives blackened*
> *by bad ways. You feel for them too…* ("Compassion" 37)

In a way, it is all about a certain mode of attention. In fact, what Vedánta Déshika means by Compassion is very often precisely God's faculty of paying attention, which definitely cannot be taken for granted. God is often inattentive, or asleep, or looking the other way (103, 83), while the poet-devotee fruitlessly tries to attract his eye. The role of Compassion is to make God take notice: she bends his glances to the devotees (19); he is equipped with eyes but she gives him sight (20); she makes him "see and think and all the rest" (82) and so on (see also 42, 98, 100, 101). Of course, God's inattention is also sometimes a blessing, another manifestation of his Compassion. We are often only too grateful if he turns a blind eye to our endless faults (e.g., 8, 63, 88). What the poet seeks and repeatedly praises, then, is God's ability to suspend, at least momentarily, the entire apparatus of judgment, while opening himself up to the helpless devotee and taking him or her in. This particular and somewhat complex quality of attentiveness is something that the poet also tries to cultivate in himself. It is also what he expects from Compassion, as the central quality of God.

The very idea that God's Compassion/attention is readily available to human beings, despite their evident lack of worthiness, is one of the central paradoxes thematized by this poem. There are others. For example, Compassion, in theory, is a mere aspect of God, but she is consistently portrayed as containing, mastering, and directing him: he takes his orders from her (24), is under her thumb (63), all his other parts are her porters and slaves (71), she is an astonishingly condensed version of God's best and truest nature:

... take the entire essence
of the God on Bull Hill
in all his immensity,
double it,
then double it again,
and you'll get
a single drop of Compassion.
("Compassion" 61, see also 22).

This infinite power ascribed to Compassion makes her predilection for helping or saving us—often from ourselves—even more incomprehensible. It is as if, the poet tells us, an untilled land had suddenly produced a yield, rich beyond imagining (20)—or as if the most miserable creature on earth suddenly found himself, thanks to Compassion, the richest person in the world (51, see also 10, 14, 39, 44, 56 etc.). Such things should not happen. In fact, there is something almost impudent, even shameless, about a Goddess so irresponsibly responsive: "It's all a game for you and, shameless, / you keep on breaking / the rules." (63)

This unruly quality of Compassion achieves its boldest expression in a series of verses that depict her as a voracious, volatile village goddess. Like other such goddesses familiar to us from modern ethnographic studies, Vedánta Déshika's Compassion is driven by her own insatiable desire, in this case her appetite for the darkest stuff of human misdeeds. And surprisingly, this need of hers serves the poet's own desperate need to unload his burden:

Look at me. I'm the worst of the worst.
If you look to others, with their meager supply of flaws,
how will you survive?
Compassion! Even a hoard of hard-core sins
hardly fills your belly. ("Compassion" 29)

First there is longing. Then, Mother,
my heart wants only to please you,
and I offer everything I have—all
my major crimes. You lick them clean,
Compassion, held close by the god
on Bull Hill, and still you're far
from satisfied, hungry
for more. ("Compassion" 97)

At the heart of Vedánta Déshika's poetic vision we thus find a stunning oxymoron—actually several staggered oxymora—configuring God's deepest persona as a merciless Compassion (26). In yet a further twist, intensifying this apparent contradiction, the devotee actively begs the goddess to show her compassion by being merciless to him, overcoming his natural tendency to flee from her:

I run away from you, Compassion.
You've got to trap me, right here
on Bull Hill. Take the Mountain King's
favorite game as your excuse. With the fibers
of his being, weave yourself into a net—
immensely strong and endlessly wide,
wide enough for every living being—
and throw yourself around
this wild animal. ("Compassion" 95)

As one modern South Indian commentator says, the poet envisions himself as a fiercely destructive creature who will do everything he can to claw his way out of the net that he has so insistently begged the goddess to cast over him.[14] And for her part, the goddess is a wild huntress, combing Bull Hill for prey. Such is the nature of this particular kind of Compassion—capricious, self-driven, even in some sense dangerous. Indeed, one good oxymoron deserves another. Faced with precisely this existential option, the poet can only ask, at the culmination of his prayer, that Compassion take him and bind him with the "iron shackles" of her mercy (99).

Capricious, self-driven, inexorable, dangerous—these same adjectives could also apply to Vedánta Déshika's sense of himself as a poet and to the kind of poetry he writes, as one sees clearly from the metapoetic epilogue to the text. A certain humble pose masks an amazingly audacious sense of accomplishment: the poet has achieved something that the "beginningless Vedas" have not even begun, perhaps have not even conceived. In fact, one intended effect of the entire poem is apparently to manipulate Compassion to the point where she has no choice but to be compassionate and to bear with "his reckless ravings" (102). These ravings reflect or express his primary experience of being overwhelmed or, more precisely, flooded: Vedánta Déshika's most common image of Compassion herself is of a massive deluge, bursting all bounds and leveling all differences. The boldness of the poet consists of his willingness to open himself up to this unruly, even violent force, in fact, to throw himself into the depths, risking his own life and sanity. His reward is to see directly into the core of God's being, which even the scriptures failed to fathom, let alone his poet predecessors:

Take all those classical poets—from Valmíki on.
They came all the way up
to a vast ocean of experience,
the experience that is you,
but they never even dipped their toes.
Compassion: shouldn't you pay me
some attention? I jumped in,
I can't touch bottom,
I'm drowning, and God
sits there smiling. ("Compassion" 103)

Make no mistake. These are highly crafted poems, replete with the entire arsenal of polished literary devices available to the "classical poets." They also lend themselves, by their lyrical nature, to crafted musical performance.[15] Nonetheless, the poet's (disingenuous?) depiction of the creative process exactly reproduces his vision of Compassion as a raging flood washing through him—as if he had no conscious agency or plan, or as if God had "taken up some lute that was lying around and, just for fun, produced a few notes" (104). The resulting poem is in itself an act of inexplicable compassion, another paradoxical gift, this time of the highest wisdom to "a mere child" (104). This gift of poetry is remembered as a disorderly rush, beyond the poet's control, and almost too rich for his readers to contain:

> *. . . Don't think I put these poems*
> *in any special order. They came*
> *tumbling out in a single fierce moment.*
> *A hurricane smashed against the wishing tree*
> *that is called "God's intention," that is nothing*
> *but Compassion, and all the mangos*
> *came crashing down.* ("Compassion" 107)

Clearly, both the "Mission of the Goose" and "Compassion" are highly complex poems that repay close attention. If you happen to know some of the intertexts, so much the better. We have tried to demonstrate some of the modes of complexity, both aesthetic and conceptual, that operate throughout these works, though we have by no means exhausted them. At the same time, like all great poetry, these works speak to us with an amazing directness and vibrancy. As we shall see, they also spoke in such ways to later generations, becoming powerful intertexts in their own right.

Appayya Díkshita: A Meditation on Self-Surrender

The final two works in this volume were composed two to three centuries later in different cultural milieux and to a different god. The two poets come from the same famous scholarly family and, in fact, knew one another; Appayya Díkshita (1520–1592), the author of "Self-Surrender" (*Ātmārpaṇastuti*), was the granduncle and teacher of Nila·kantha Díkshita (1580–1644), who composed "Peace" (*Śāntivilāsa*). Appayya was one of India's leading intellectuals in the sixteenth century. He was an important innovator in the traditions of Vedic Hermeneutics (*Mīmāṃsā*), *Vedānta*, and Sanskrit Poetics (*Alaṃkāra / śāstra*), whose scholarship attracted admirers and critics throughout the subcontinent. The celebrated grammarian Bhattóji Díkshita, for instance, came all the way from Varánasi to study with Appayya at his home village of Adaya·palam, in the north Tamil country, while the renowned Jagan·natha, "King of Pundits" at the Mughal court of Shah Jahan, dedicated a whole book to criticizing his views on poetics. Yet besides his "all-India" scholarly status, Appayya was deeply involved in the local scene of the South during the late Víjaya·nágara era. He was associated with several local rajas, built a temple in his native village, wrote hymns for local deities; to this day, his image is carved and painted in several South Indian temples and monastic schools.

In terms of his philosophical orientation, Appayya was a *Śiv'/âdvaitin*, in the line of the philosophy of oneness that goes back to the great Shánkaracharya, but with a strong Shaiva coloring—that is, the language he uses is linked to the worship of Shiva. This puts him, ostensibly, in a different camp from Vedánta Déshika, particularly at a time when sectarian boundaries were becoming far more rigid and when Appayya himself was in competition with Vedánta Déshika's Shri Vaishnava heirs. Nonetheless, we know that Appayya was a great admirer of Vedánta Déshika: he authored the sole existing commentary on Vedánta Déshika's poetic magnum opus, the *Yādavābhyudaya*, and paid tribute to his oeuvre in a variety of ways (he may have even written a commentary, now lost, on the *Haṃsasandeśa*). Indeed, despite his strong Shaiva affiliation, Appayya's position on sectarian issues was more complex than what we see in later hagiographic literature about him.

Like Vedánta Déshika, Appayya was both a philosopher and a poet, though perhaps more a philosopher than a poet. His poetry consisted entirely of hymns to a variety of divinities, to most of which he has attached a self-composed commentary, and which often bear a resemblance to scholarly essays or public sermons.[16] Among these hymns, "Self-Surrender" has a certain salience in the eyes of the tradition, as one sees by a story that the tradition has attached to it. According to this framing narrative, Appayya once informed his disciples that he had taken a hallucinatory substance made of the juice of the datura plant in order to test his devotion to Shiva. He requested his students to remain attentive and write down whatever he uttered during his trance. What came out of his mouth were the fifty verses of "Self-Surrender" (Ramesan 1972: 113). Thus this poem, alone in the vast corpus of Appayya, is seen as emerging from an altered state of consciousness, triggered by datura, but expressing a mode of heightened inspiration and intensified perception. Note that this *stotra*, unlike most of his other such works, comes to us without a self-authored commentary. On the one hand this fact signals the author's intimate and direct dialogue with God, if not between two aspects or parts of a single identity. On the other hand, as the story itself indicates, the moment of Appayya's verbal surrender has a public dimension built into it.

One could say that the whole poem is centered around the author's announcement, a profoundly consequential speech-act found in verses 15–17, of his total surrender to Shiva. The formula he uses in each of these three verses is the first person verb *prapadye*, literally "I take refuge," "surrender," or "give my self," to "you," that is God in the second person. As an abstract noun this verb gives us the forms *prapatti* or *prapadana*, which evoke the Shri Vaishnava ideal discussed earlier. Indeed, Appayya has effectively appropriated this terminology and the devotional practice it signifies for a Shaiva context. This is not the only example of such cross-fertilization over sectarian boundaries in Appayya's works. Consider, for example, his depiction of the gods as "waiting a long long time," singing god's praises at his doorstep, and of himself, "no better than a worm," who nonetheless expects God

... to answer
my prayers right away. I'm truly wretched
and I know I can count
on your kindness. ("Self-Surrender" 21)

Readers of Vedánta Déshika's "Compassion" will immediately feel at home, recognizing a familiar paradox: the lower the better. Only a worm-like creature can have the confidence (*viśvāsa*) of winning God's immediate attention, when even the highest gods have to wait indefinitely. The underlying logic of this assumption, again familiar to us from the intertext, is that the human speaker is so much in need and so utterly without hope or other options that the god has no choice but to save him.

Indeed, these two texts are closely interrelated, and we have no doubt that Appayya took "Compassion" as at least a partial model for his "Self-Surrender." There are unmistakable echoes of the former in the latter. These include the repeated request that the deity take upon himself the devotee's burdens, both past and future (12, 25), and the oxymoronic images of God as simultaneously both "lock and key" (*īśvaro bandha/muktyoḥ*, 24), or as supplying a lock which is, in fact, the only key to freedom:

> *Couldn't you tie us to the yoke*
> *of knowledge, so we can untie*
> *our knots?* ("Self-Surrender" 25)

This is taken directly from Vedánta Déshika, with his burning appeal to Compassion to trap him.

However, what has been edited out in this theological translation to Appayya's peculiar strand of Shaivism is the sense of Compassion as a living, voracious goddess with her own moods and her desperate hunger for sins. Instead of the bloodthirsty games of Compassion the huntress, we have Shiva's unpredictable games and guises, played out in the burning grounds together with his rowdy gang of *gaṇas*. Beyond this, there is a whole new theology of Shiva as the supreme deity, to whom all other gods are subordinate (1–5, 17–18, 25, 35, 42–44), and who is at the same time the highest principle, the Vedantic *ātman*, or universal self. This identification somewhat unexpectedly makes God the speaker's own innermost self. Thus the very title of the work, *Ātmārpaṇa*, contains a certain ambiguity which reflects a deep tension in the very act of self-surrender—we have the surrender of the self to the self. This tension is, indeed, thematized repeatedly throughout the text, often in surprising ways.

We see this dialectic in the first full-throated declaration of submission:

Now is the time.
I'm at your feet.
I take my self and offer it,
together with everyone around me,
to Myself,
that is, to You, Lord … ("Self-Surrender" 15)

One clear element is the vast gap between the speaker's two selves, one of which can never understand the other. Strangely, however, this very gap is the condition of intimate self-experience, or indeed self-knowledge, the special medicine (*sv'|ātma|bodh'|āuṣadha*) for healing the "disease called life" (18). Thus the transition from first person to second person pronoun and back is somewhat misleading. These transitions take place within some inner, private space. At the same time, the act of surrender itself is not only attended by Appayya's students, if we are to believe the framing narrative, but also expands to include "everyone around me." As we will see below, in the section on

Nila·kantha Díkshita, a later generation would find itself directly implied by this reference.

At any rate, the main paradox at work is the surrender of one thing to itself so that the giving of the self is, inevitably, the full coming into self. Unexpected forms of barter and exchange result from this odd dynamic. The divine recipient of one's self-surrender can only hold it in deposit pending the moment when it is withdrawn, and there is always the suspicion that God will consume, or take for himself, what belongs to, or indeed is, the self that has been offered. A weird asymmetry, perhaps masking a deeper symmetry, can lead to complaints such as the following:

You play the beggar's roles to perfection,
but really, Father, you're eating up in secret
our common store of pleasures, depriving me
of my rightful share. You're the leader
of all worlds. You set the boundaries. Tell me,
is this a fair allocation? Give me back
myself and we'll be partners
again. ("Self-Surrender" 35)

It would be possible to restate such propositions in the lucid philosophical language that Appayya elsewhere developed, for example in "An Iota of Truth" (*Siddhāntaleśa*) and "Sunstone of Shaivism" (*Śivārkamaṇidīpaka*). As McCrea (2006) has shown, Appayya has in effect invented a new Shaiva theology and supplied it retrospectively with a Vedantic history. A further exploration of these themes would take us far beyond the literary contours of the text we have translated here.

One thing more, however, has to be said about the personal quality of these internal interactions. If one reads through the text from beginning to end, a certain progression becomes apparent. The first verses lead up to the moment of surrender in a rather logical pattern. The poem begins by describing Shiva's greatness (1–5), turns to the "I" and its utter failure to attain Shiva (6–12), and predicts a similar failure at the moment of death, despite the conventional hope that one might focus awareness on God at this crucial time and thus attain release (13–14). Then comes the decisive cry of surrender, in three verses that echo, indeed rhyme with one another (15–17). By rights, the poem should have ended here. Instead, the great moment of transformation is followed by a long trail of afterthoughts, seemingly chaotic and restless. It is almost as if Appayya is not completely certain about his own act, and in the following verses he alternates between the advaita ideal of an indistinguishable merger with god in the form of the universal Self (34–35, 40, 42–43), and the bhakta's desire to be reborn in order to remain god's servant (19–20, 36–37, 45), sometimes in the very same verse (47).

Nonetheless, we can see that the act of surrender has truly changed the speaker. The expressive "I" is no longer the same once it has offered itself to its Self. For one thing, a kind of intimacy, bold and imaginative, is established between the human and divine parts of the same person. For another thing, while the anxieties that drove that poet to his desperate act have not disappeared, he feels confident enough to make repeated demands on the god. Something also changes in the way he imagines the all-important moment of his death. The same situation obtains—a terror-filled crowd of relatives surrounding the dying self, sick and suffering while breathing his last—but this time he seems to believe that he will manage to transcend this most difficult moment in his life and find himself:

Death is here. Watching what's left of my life—
my last breaths, fluttering in my throat—
my loved ones, wailing, terrified
that the end has come, close in on me,
while within I suffer endlessly,
blow after blow. Now, even now,
I pray to Myself, who is you,
to let my self come to rest
at your feet. ("Self-Surrender" 38, see also 39)

And it's not only the thoughts about death that have been significantly altered. A certain insouciance makes itself heard—as if the poet, who earlier claimed not to be able to fathom God, were suddenly so sure of himself that he can even see through the conventional guises of Shiva, knowing him in a visionary mode within. And this vision has a stable quality within the general field of restlessness, which seems, in itself, to be inherent to the post-prapatti situation. The speaker even promises the internalized Self: "…From now on I'll never let go/ even in my sleep of your/ two lotus feet." (42)

This assertion comes right before the poet switches gears, changing the meter for the first time—from the stately *mandākrāntā*, that sometimes serves for highly personal statements—in order to signal that the poem is coming to its conclusion. The final verses, in various meters, constitute a strong metapoetic statement, such as we saw in Vedánta Déshika's "Compassion." Such self-reflexive conclusions, always including an apology for the assumed artistic failure of the work, if not for the act of composing it, may even be a stable feature of this genre of medieval Sanskrit stotras. In Appayya's case, the last verse, serving as a colophon signed by the author, actually disclaims responsibility for the extraordinary contents of all the preceding forty-nine verses:

So much for "Self-Surrender."
It's not as if I composed it
with a focused mind. Still,
just say to yourself:
"This poor excuse for a man
is only asking for shelter,
muttering mere words."
God rich in compassion:
please look after me. ("Self-Surrender" 50)

The reader should compare this with the final verses of "Compassion," with their images of the poet as a passive musical instrument in the hands of God, or of the poem as a result of an unstoppable hurricane hitting against the Wishing Tree of Compassion. In Appayya's concluding verse, by contrast, the poet imagines what God might say to himself about his work—that however awkward the words may seem, generated in some altered state of consciousness, as the story tells us, they must be excused because of the genuine impulse they embody, and because God is, after all, "rich in compassion."

Nila·kantha Díkshita: The Skeptic's Search for Peace

There is a story that at the age of twelve, Nila·kantha received from his dying granduncle and teacher, Appayya, several of the latter's most cherished belongings. Among the items were the *Śiva/liṅgam*s that Appayya worshiped, his personal rosary, and two books: the "Celebration of the Goddess" (*Devīmāhātmya*) and Kali·dasa's *Raghuvaṃśa*. On this occasion Appayya is said to have predicted Nila·kantha's successful career as a minister of the king of Madurai, in the far south. Nila·kantha then went to Madurai and started lecturing on the *Devīmāhātmya*. Coming to the notice of the king, Tiru·malai Náyaka, through these discourses, Nila·kantha was appointed, as prophesied, to be his minister (BRONNER 2007: 7). This, then, is the story of a prolific poet, who also played a major role in the political arena of his time. Among his major works are sustained narrative *kāvya*s such as the masterful "Black-Neck's Victory" (*Nīlakaṇṭhavijayacampū*), supposedly composed when he was still a boy, the "Descent of the Ganges" (*Gaṅgāvataraṇa*), the "Ocean of Shiva's Tricks" (*Śivalīlārṇava*, retelling, in Sanskrit, the stories of Shiva's sixty-four amusements in Madurai), as well as a long series of satirical, lyrical, and liturgical works.

Another story depicts Nila·kantha's last days in the service of his king. They say that during the construction of the Pudu·mándapam compound in the Madurai temple, under the supervision of Nila·kantha, a sculptor was working on images of the king and his queen. A tiny stone chip mysteriously slipped away from the image of the queen's left thigh.

The horrified sculptor was about to repair the image when Nila·kantha stopped him, saying that the chipless hip corresponded exactly to the original, and that the queen had a mole at that intimate spot. The king, hearing of this, immediately suspected the worst and sent his soldiers to tear out Nila·kantha's eyes. As they arrived, Nila·kantha was performing *pūjā* to Minákshi, the goddess of Madurai; divining the purpose of the troops' arrival, he took the burning camphor he was using for worship and burnt out his eyes himself. When this was reported to the king, he realized his mistake and rushed to throw himself at his minister's feet and beg his forgiveness. But even before he arrived, Nila·kantha had completed composing and singing a hymn to Minákshi, the "Hymn to the Ocean of Joy" (*Ānandasāgara-stava*), at the end of which the goddess appeared and restored his sight. Despite the king's pleas, Nila·kantha was now determined to resign his post and spend the remainder of his life in the small village of Pala·madai, where he sang the praises of God (FILLIOZAT 1967: 4–6).

Note that this story, or close variants of it, are also attached to several other figures. For our purposes, however, the story resonates with an explicit theme, or tone, of "Peace"—the world-weary rejection of society, including kingship and politics. As it stands, the story beautifully embodies the cultural opposition between two ideal-types of poets—one at home in the royal court, the other praising God in his temple (NARAYANA RAO 1992; BRONNER & SHULMAN 2006: 2–5). Whether or not Nila·kantha truly made the transition from one mode to the other, his poem betrays his deep skepticism about the joys of an intellectual's life at court:

All the trouble I took,
ever since I was a kid
serving at the feet of my teachers,
to fathom the secrets of God—
look what came out of it:
the stuff of bedtime stories
that I tell yawning kings,
night after night,
to kill time. ("Peace" 8)

The bitterly ironic tone, a trademark of the entire work, is even more pointed in an earlier verse on kingship and other political realities:

If you have the great good fortune,
of making friends with the king's close aides,
you've found your guru.
If they let you past the gate,
you're in heaven.
Then, if you get to meet the king in person,
it'll be like shaking God's hand.
And if you drop dead at your post in the palace,
as far as I'm concerned,
that's instant
redemption. ("Peace" 6)

Irony is too crude a term for the complex and subtle tones that dominate this introspective and strangely modern work. The poet's voice is entirely distinctive, indeed unmistakable once you have read a few verses. "Peace" begins with a clear and poignant statement of the poet's failure to attain peace:

What a family to be born into! Can you believe
who turned out to be my parents?
And all the lectures I've heard—the finest professors,
the range of topics, class after class…
I've seen how bad the world can be. Tasted
every pleasure. What I've never managed
is a quiet heart. As you can see,
I've got it made. ("Peace" 1)

Listen to the self-deprecating conclusion. It is quite true that Nila·kantha was born into an unusually gifted brahmin family, made famous by his granduncle Appayya. It is true that he must have had a superb education. But what he lacks, by his own repeated testimony, is that happy peacefulness that the classical tradition holds out as an ideal for the pious. In fact, it is not even clear that Nila·kantha really aspired to that ideal, for he comes through as deeply skeptical—even about the religious precepts and doctrines that inform this ideal.

At first glance, these highly personal and rather sober verses call to mind the whole genre of poems preaching dispassion (*vairāgya*), beginning perhaps with the great fifth-century poet Bhartri·hari. The latter's "Three Hundred Poems" (*Śatakatraya*)[17] reveals another strong individual voice, also skeptical at times, but utterly torn between the incompatible attractions of sexual passion and the relief of escaping from it. To take a random example:

Why waste so many words? Who needs all these
empty lectures? It's clear that a man always has
only two choices: he can go for the wildness
of sexy young women, staggering under the weight
of their breasts, reinventing the meaning of passion
with every slow step, or he can go off
to the wilderness.[18]
(*Śatakatraya* of Bhartri·hari, *Śṛṅgāraśataka* 85)

It might seem that one of the two options, or poles, has a certain advantage in the poet's eyes, though other verses of the *Śatakatraya* shift the balance in the opposite direction. At any rate, in Bhartri·hari's poetry, one gets the full blast of his conflicted soul. But Nila·kantha, by contrast, is in no way committed to rejecting the world or to a simple notion of release. He is as skeptical about this idea as about everything else. His tone is confessional, intimate, self-ironic and reflective, softer than Bhartri·hari's, softer even than Appayya's own self-deprecation in his "Self-Surrender." Take for example any of the many verses in "Peace" that deal with sex. The poet has been there, has tasted it all. He is neither disgusted with it nor is he in the grip of insatiable desire. He tells us that he has reached a point in his life where

The fire that was burning in my gut
has flickered out.
My love life
is a faded rumor. ("Peace" 12)

It is as if Nila·kantha has seen through passion and regards it with a kind of wry detachment. Again and again he offers a down-to-earth economy of human emotions: love has its ups and downs, and sometimes even the most passionate of lovers need a vacation before they can resume full-fledged lovemaking (27); whores can be very attractive but making love to them is not so different from what one does with one's wife (28); and anyway, the whole business has a slightly silly aspect, putting humans on a par with other animals (18, 30). Indeed, "business" may be exactly the right word for this sort of give and take (see, for example, verse 3).

A somewhat mercenary tone, in fact, pervades the work. There is a recurring set of metaphors based on hardnosed calculation. Life consists of good and (mostly) bad investments; people generally make irrational decisions, often based on a foolish niggardliness and on a failure to recognize what really matters (7, 29). So conspicuous is this economic perspective on the world that we are tempted to see it as the natural expression of a rising urban middle-level elite, such as we know to have existed in an increasingly monetarized seventeenth-century South India (NARAYANA RAO, SHULMAN & SUBRAHMANYAM 2001: 93–139). Consider the following example:

Our life's savings—all that hard work!—
we risk it all when we come across
some scrap of paper promising a profit
of one percent. But when it comes to the life
beyond, where the profits in store are
a thousand times more (so the scriptures
ensure), we're so obsessed with overspending
that we won't risk
a single penny. ("Peace" 19)

This calculus of physical and metaphysical advantage feeds into the skeptical worldview that we have been discussing. More precisely, Nila·kantha consistently ridicules this all-too-human propensity for petty reckoning based on very narrowly conceived self-interest. He wants more than this out of life, though he is not at all sure that he, weak human being that he is, is capable of rising above such habits.

Somewhat surprisingly, this particular reflective brand of skepticism expands to include the whole richly elaborated realm of religious life and norms that come under the rubric of dharma. Vows, fasts, pilgrimages, charity, acts of repentance, the whole gamut of daily and seasonal rites (which require tremendous effort and tend to be costly!), and, for that matter, the scriptures themselves, which enjoin all of these, together with the dharma books—in the end they all add up to very little when seen in the light of the overwhelming presence of death. Indeed, these texts seem almost oblivious to the simple, horrible, and imminent reality of dying:

> *"First, study the Veda.*
> *Then build a home.*
> *Make money.*
> *Perform the rituals.*
> *Father children.*
> *Then, at the end of your life,*
> *set out for the forest."*
> *Sounds good. I'm all for it, if only*
> *Manu, or Yajna·valkya, or whoever said it,*
> *can guarantee exactly how long*
> *I have to live.* ("Peace" 39)

This may sound like earlier voices in the tradition urging people to renounce the world at once in order to escape the endless suffering built into existence. But in fact, the thrust of Nila·kantha's verses is entirely different. First, there is the underlying skepticism and, in fact, active disbelief that we have already mentioned. In a verse deliberately echoing the opening of the text, cited above, he confesses that despite all his congenital gifts and advantages, he sees no spiritual hope for himself:

... If after all this, in this best
of all possible lives,
I still can't bring myself
to believe, how will I ever
be free? Even if everyone else
is released, I'll still be stuck here,
in hell. ("Peace" 47)

Secondly, this poet is anguished by the inescapable brute extinction of his irreplaceable individual awareness, as we will see in a moment.

Thirdly, the whole discussion of death, perhaps the leitmotif of the poem as a whole, has a fresh quality, again almost modern and familiar. Adjectives like "honest," "humorous," "humane," "unflinching," come to mind. He simply will not turn away his glance from the empirical observation, which he knows well from his own experience, that people inevitably turn away their glance from death:

Death's messengers?
How will they ever find me,
lying in my hole?

Suppose they do find me,
what can they do?
They won't mess with me.
Suppose they do try something?
I'll put the king on their case
right away. I'm much too important
to think about dying. ("Peace" 14)

When it comes to dying, denial is our default (see also verses 9–11, 15, 17, 20, 38, 40).

You might think that some kind of simpleminded appeal to God is the answer to all this doubt and anxiety. But the fact is that Shiva is, at best, a rather passive onlooker, overhearing from a distance the poet's internal monologue. Unlike in Appayya's "Self-Surrender," with its constant and intimate dialogue with the god, here Shiva hardly enters the conversation—until the very last, powerful verses. This is because even God himself is not immune to the dominant skeptical stance. Moreover, Nila·kantha's god has limited powers, especially when it comes to helping us human beings, who do not really want to be helped (36, 41). Given these constraints on both the skeptical devotee and his not-so-omnipotent god, a certain creative inventiveness offers the only slight hope for a happy ending. Nila·kantha thus attempts to negotiate with Shiva, and he takes it upon himself to suggest to Shiva another way to infiltrate him into heaven:

Your heaven is packed with pure souls...
Wouldn't you like to show them, just once,
something new, something they've never ever seen,

a truly stupid creature?
That way you can take me
to your city
beyond this world. ("Peace" 46)

In the end, the one thing Nila·kantha has going for him is his uniquely abysmal inadequacy. Indeed, he challenges Shiva to find "anywhere in this world, someone like me" (44)—he seems almost to take a perverse pride in being "an ocean of mindlessness," as if this were the defining feature of his humanity. Nila·kantha did not invent this theme; we find exactly parallel passages in the fifteenth-century Telugu poet Annamacharya, or Annamayya, from Tirupati (Narayana Rao & Shulman 2005: 27).

Clearly we have come a long way from Vedánta Déshika's burning faith and theology of compassion; also from Appayya Díkshita's trance of self-surrender. Nila·kantha belongs to a different time, a different social reality, and a different metaphysical sensibility. To fully appreciate this newness, we have to come to terms with the final verses of "Peace," where Shiva is finally invoked in a more direct and urgent manner, just as Nila·kantha makes himself present in a fully personal and individual way. He reminds the god of his former promises to Nila·kantha's own family (50), as he does also in his *Ānandasāgarastava*, where the reference to Appayya's collective surrender is made explicit.[19] Then he articulates a vision, perhaps never before seen in Sanskrit poetry, of a kind of happiness, or indeed, peace, that is not universal, certainly not the Vedantic fallback model, and may not even be what we would call "religious":

I'm not asking for the moon,
Indra's throne, or Brahma's heaven,
let alone some other galaxy.
What place is left for you if you want to be
someone else? All I'm asking for,
Shiva,
is that gentle feeling
that is mine. ("Peace" 49)

Gone are the joys of total, undifferentiated consciousness, of becoming pure light, of deathless awareness, of uniting one's self with the Ultimate. What Nila·kantha seeks is a more modest, yet at the same time more humanly accessible goal, this *masṛṇitaṃ māmakānandam*, a softness just right for him.

The four works presented in this volume are but a tiny sample of the poems and prayers in Southern Sanskrit, to say nothing of the vast parallel canons in Tamil, Telugu, Kannada, and Malayalam. We have offered a few analytical suggestions meant to differentiate the three poets from one another and also to establish the direct links between them. Among the issues we have mentioned only in passing are those related to the peculiar expressive properties of medieval Sanskrit, at least in this southern domain. Anyone who comes to these works with a knowledge of Tamil, most likely the mother tongue of all three poets, cannot help but notice the sustained impact of Tamil speech and Tamil literary modes. There is much to be said about the syntactic specificity of the poetry as well as linguistic features such as modality and aspectuality, with which Tamil, and a slightly Tamilized Sanskrit, are richly endowed. In some of the works, especially in Nila·kantha Díkshita's "Peace," there are clear echoes of colloquial, idiomatic speech—a supple, succulent Sanskrit, which contemporary readers undoubtedly enjoyed for its freshness. This language was certainly alive and kicking for these brahmin authors and their readers. We should always bear in mind, moreover, that these poets, as SHELDON POLLOCK has often stressed, made a choice by composing in Sanskrit. All three of them could have written poetry in Tamil and perhaps in Telugu as well. That they nonetheless opted for Sanskrit, a Sanskrit suffused by echoes of earlier Sanskrit classics as well as of the vernacular canons, indicates a lively poetic scene in which Sanskrit offered something new and unique.

The happy experience of translating these poems together kept us busy for two years in various settings and circumstances—mostly in Chicago, Jerusalem, and Kollapuram. We'd like to thank all those who made it possible and indeed pleasant for us to work for long hours: Katikaneni Vimala, who hosted us in her village; the Institute of Advanced Studies at the Hebrew University, which provided a space in which we first began to explore the question of regional Sanskrit in 2005, and which continued to support our work under optimal conditions; the Department of South Asian Languages and Civilizations at the University of Chicago; Café Smadar in the German Colony and Café Shosh in Katamon, in Jerusalem; the hospitable Jerusalem Hotel in East Jerusalem; and Galila and Eileen, who exemplified the virtue of *kṣamā*, or forbearance. We are also grateful to Oscar Figueroa, who helped type in the transliterated texts, and Velcheru Narayana Rao, who read a draft of the translation and made insightful comments. H.V. Nagaraja Rao shed light on several verses of "Peace." We thank Isabelle Onians, Chris Gibbons, and Dániel Balogh of the CSL team for their meticulous and selfless editing.

Notes

1 On this point we differ from POLLOCK's views, as expressed in POLLOCK (2003) and, more mildly, in POLLOCK (2006: 572).

2 For an overview of Vedánta Déshika's works, see HOPKINS (2002) and SINGH (1958).

3 For a recent translation, see the volume in the Clay Sanskrit Library by SIR JAMES MALLINSON (2006).

4 A structural analysis of the genre was given by the anonymous Kerala author of the *Śukasandeśavyākṛti*, and expanded by Dharmagupta in his commentary to the *Śukasandeśa*. See the introduction by N.P. UNNI to the *Meghasandeśa* of Kali·dasa, 16–17.

5 - - - - ˘ ˘ ˘ ˘ ˘ - - ˘ - - ˘ - -

6 *dhūmajyotiḥsalilamarutāṃ saṃnipātaḥ kva meghaḥ*
sandeśārthāḥ kva paṭukaraṇaiḥ prāṇibhiḥ prāpaṇīyāḥ
ity autsukyād aparigaṇayan guhyakas taṃ yayāce
kāmārtā hi prakṛtikṛpaṇāś cetanācetaeṣu.

7 See *Meghasandeśa* 1.22, 1.32.

8 *saiṣā sthalī yatra vicinvatā tvāṃ*
bhraṣṭaṃ mayā nūpuram ekam ūrvyām

adṛṣyata tvac/caraṇāravinda/
viśleṣa/duḥkhād iva baddha-maunam.

9 This contrasting temporality is nicely stated by the modal *upadheyam*—the left anklet "should be tied" by Rama in the hoped for, envisaged future.

10 See BRONNER & SHULMAN (2006) for a broader discussion of density or depth.

11 *aṅgenāṅgaṃ pratanu tanunā gāḍhataptena taptaṃ*
sāsreṇāśrudrutam aviratotkaṇṭham utkaṇṭhitena
uṣṇocchvāsaṃ samadhikatarocchvāsinā dūravartī
saṃkalpais tair viśati vidhinā vairiṇā ruddhamārgaḥ.

12 *Śrīraṅgamāhātmya* 7–9.

13 *Meghasandeśa* 2.40.

14 See our note on our translation of that verse.

15 See, for example, T.M. KRISHNA's rendition of two verses from the *Dayāśataka* in *Toḍi rāga*: Kṣetra Tirupati, Charsur, Chennai 2002.

16 See BRONNER (2007), where "Self-Surrender" is discussed.

17 Translated by GREG BAILEY in *Love Lyrics*, Clay Sanskrit Library, 2005.

18 *kim iha bahubhir uktair yuktiśūnyaiḥ pralāpair*
dvayam iha puruṣāṇāṃ sarvadā sevanīyam
abhinava-mada-līlā-lālasaṃ sundarīṇāṃ
stana-bhara-parikhinnaṃ yauvanaṃ vā vanaṃ vā.

19 *Ānandasāgarastava*, verse 43, cf. Bronner (2007).

Bibliographic Notes

A word about the editions that served as our base texts: For the *Haṃsasandeśa*, we mostly used the Madras 1955 edition, edited with commentary by SWETARANYAM NARAYANA SASTRY. For the *Dayāśataka*: the Madras 1970 edition by NALLŪR ŚRĪNIVĀSA RĀGHAVĀCĀRYA SVĀMI. For the *Ātmārpaṇastuti*: the Secunderabad 1980 edition, by A. RAMAKRISHNA DIKSHITHAR and K. RAMACHANDRA SARMA. For the *Śāntivilāsa*: the 1943 Madras edition, backed up by FILLIOZAT (1967). We have noted variant readings of more than trivial significance from the other editions of these works, which are listed in the bibliography.

PRIMARY SOURCES

Ātmārpaṇastuti of [Dikshitendra] Appayya Dīkṣita. In *Collection of Stotras by Srimad Appayya Dikshitendra with Own Commentaries*, edited by A. RAMAKRISHNA DIKSHITHAR and K. RAMACHANDRA SARMA. Vol. 3, Srimad Appayya Dikshitendra Granthavali. Secunderabad: Srimad Appayya Dikshitendra Granthavali, 1980.

Ātmārpaṇastuti of Appayya Dīkṣita. With commentaries in Sanskrit and Hindi by ŚRĪŚAṄKARANĀRĀYAṆA. Varanasi: Kṛṣṇadāsa Akādamī, 1982.

Ānandasāgarastava of Nīlakaṇṭha Dīkṣita. Mysore: Sudharmā Prakāśanam. 1999.

Dayāśataka of Vedānta Deśika. Edited with Tamil commentary by NALLŪR ŚRĪNIVĀSA RĀGHAVĀCĀRYA SVĀMI. Madras, Visishtadvaita Pracharini Sabha, 1970.

Śrītayāśatakam of Vedāntatēśika: mutal pākam, 60 ślōkaṅkaḷ. Srirangam: Srimad Andavan Poundarikapuram Swami Asramam, 2007.

Dayāśataka of Vedānta Deśika. With Telugu commentary by K. ŚAṬHAGOPĀCĀRYULU. Tirupati, Tirumala Tirupati Devasthanam Press, 1982.

Śrī Vedānta Deśika's Stotras with English Translation. By S.S. RAGHAVAN, M.S. LAKSHMI KUMARI, and M. NARASIMHACHARY. Madras, Sripad Trust. 1995.

Haṃsasandeśa of Vedānta Deśika. With commentary by RANGA CHARIAR. Notes and translation by N.V. DESIKA CHARIAR and KASTURI RANGA AYENGAR. Madras: Vedanta Desika Research Society, 1973.

Haṃsasandeśa of Vedānta Deśika. Edited with commentary by SWETARANYAM NARAYANA SASTRY, English notes and translation by S. NARAYANA IYENGAR, Madras, 1955.

Haṃsasandeśa of Vedānta Deśika. Edited with commentary by UTTAMUR T. VIRARAGHAVACHARYA. Madras, Visishtadvaita Pracharini Sabha, 1973.

Kuvalayānanda of Appayya Dīkṣita with the Hindi commentary *Alaṅkārasurabhi* of D. BHOLASHANKAR VYAS Varanasi, Chowkhamba Vidyabhawan, 1992

Meghasandeśa of Kālidāsa, with the commentaries of Dakṣiṇāvartanātha, Pūrṇasarasvati and Parameśvara. 1987. Edited by N.P. UNNI. Delhi: Bharatiya Vidya Prakashan.

Raghuvaṃśa of Kālidāsa, with the commentaries of Mallinātha and Haragovinda Śāstrī. 1985. Vol. 51, Kashi Sanskrit Series. Varanasi: Chaukhambha.

Śatakatraya of Bhartṛhari, see MILLER 1967.

Śāntivilāsa of Nīlakaṇṭha Dīkṣita. With Tamil Commentary by Y. Mahalinga Sastri. Kumbakonam, Sri Kamakoti Publishing House, 1943.

Śrīraṅgamāhātmya, edited by KUPPUSAMI AYYANGAR, Tiruccirappalli, 1908.

SECONDARY SOURCES

BRONNER, YIGAL. 2007. "Singing to God, Educating the People: Appayya Dīkṣita and the Function of Stotras." *Journal of the American Oriental Society* 127(2): 113–30.

Bronner, Yigal, and David Shulman. 2006. "A Cloud Turned Goose: Sanskrit in the Vernacular Millennium." *Indian Economic and Social History Review* 43(1): 1–30.

Filliozat, Pierre-Sylvain. 1967. *Oeuvres poétiques de Nīlakaṇṭha Dīkṣita.* Publications de l'Institut Français d'Indologie, no. 36. Pondichéry: Institut Français d'Indologie.

Hardy, Friedhelm. 1979. "The Philosopher as Poet: A Study of Vedāntadeśika's Dehalīśastuti." *Journal of Indian Philosophy* 7: 227–325.

Hiltebeitel, Alf. 1977. "Nahuṣa in the Skies: A Human King in Heaven." *History of Religions* 16: 329–50.

Hopkins, Steven Paul. 2002. *Singing the Body of God: The Hymns of Vedāntadeśika in Their South Indian Tradition.* New York: Oxford University Press.

Mallinson, James. 2006. *Messenger Poems* by Kālidāsa, Dhoyī & Rūpa Goswamin. New York: New York University Press & JJC Foundation.

McCrea, Lawrence. 2006. "Coloring Tradition: Appayya Dīkṣita's Invention of Śrīkaṇṭha's Vedānta." Paper delivered at the 35th Annual Conference on South Asia, University of Wisconsin-Madison.

Miller, Barbara Stoller. 1967. *Bhartṛhari: Poems.* New York & London. Columbia University Press.

Narayana Rao, Velcheru. 1992. "Kings, Gods, and Poets: Ideologies of Patronage in Medieval Andhra." In: Barbara Stoler Miller (ed.), *The Powers of Art: Patronage in Indian Culture*. Delhi: Oxford University Pres, 142–59.

Narayana Rao, Velcheru, and David Shulman. 2005. *God on the Hill*. New York: Oxford University Press.

Narayana Rao, Velcheru, David Shulman, and Sanjay Subrahmanyam. 2001. *Textures of Time: Writing History in South India 1600–1800*. Delhi: Permanent Black.

Pollock, Sheldon. 2003. "Sanskrit Literary Culture from the inside Out." In: Sheldon Pollock (ed.), *Literary Cultures in History:*

Reconstructions from South Asia. Berkeley: University of California Press, 39–130.

———. 2006. *The Language of the Gods in the World of Men: Sanskrit, Culture, and Power in Premodern India*. Berkeley: University of California Press.

RAMESAN, N. 1972. *Sri Appayya Diksita*. Hyderabad: Srimad Appayya Dikshitendra Granthavali Pakasana Samithi.

SINGH. 1958. *Vedāntadeśika – A Study – His Life, Works, and Philosophy*. Benaras: Chowkhamba.

Abbreviations

HSed: *Haṃsasandeśa* principal edition: S. NARAYANA IYENGAR (1955).
HSvl: *Haṃsasandeśa* variant readings noted in the principal edition, mentioned in NARAYANA SASTRY's commentary or in the English notes of NARAYANA IYENGAR.
HSalt: *Haṃsasandeśa* edited with commentary by UTTAMUR T. VIRARAGHAVACHARYA (1973).
DSed: *Dayāśataka* principal edition: NALLŪR ŚRĪNIVĀSA RĀGHAVĀCĀRYA SVĀMI (1970).
DSalt: *Dayāśataka* edited by K. ŚAṬHAGOPĀCĀRYULU (1982).
ASed: *Ātmārpaṇastuti* principal edition: A. RAMAKRISHNA DIKSHITHAR and K. RAMACHANDRA SARMA (1980).
ASvl: *Ātmārpaṇastuti* variant readings noted in the principal edition.
ASalt: *Ātmārpaṇastuti* edited by ŚRĪŚAṄKARANĀRĀYAṆA (1982).

THE MISSION OF THE GOOSE

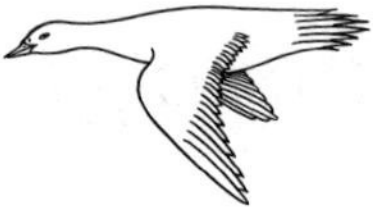

FIRST PART

1.1 VAṂŚE JĀTAḤ Savitur an|aghe,
mānayan mānuṣatvaṃ,
devaḥ Śrīmāñ Janaka|tanay"|ân-
veṣaṇe jāgarūkaḥ,
pratyāyāte Pavanatanaye
niścit'|ârthaḥ sa kāmī
kalp'|ākārāṃ katham api niśām
ā|vibhātaṃ viṣehe.

kālye senāṃ kapi|kula|pates
tūrṇam udyojayiṣyan,
dūrī|bhāvāj Janaka|duhitur
dūyamān'|ântar|ātmā,
krīḍā|khelaṃ kamala|sarasi
kv' âpi kāl'|ôpayātaṃ
rākā|candra|dyuti|saha|caraṃ
rāja|haṃsaṃ dadarśa.

tasmin Sītā|gatim anugate,
tad|dukūl'|âṅka†|mūrtau,
tan|mañjīra|pratima|ninade
nyasta|niṣpanda|dṛṣṭiḥ
vīraś ceto|vilayam agamat
tanmay'|ātmā muhūrtaṃ.

1.3 *aṅka* HSed : *anta* HSvl

Prelude

BORN IN THE flawless lineage of the Sun, 1.1
lending dignity to being human,
this god, never without Fortune,
was wide awake, eager to set off
to find Jánaka's daughter.
He was ready to go,
now that Hánuman had returned.*
Somehow or other, burning with passion,
he got through the night
that seemed to stretch on forever
until dawn.

Early in the morning, sick at heart
since Jánaka's daughter was far away,
and anxious to set in motion
the army of the monkey king,
he saw
the likeness of the full moon:
a regal goose
arrived right on time,
playing somewhere
in a lotus pond.

It walked Sita's walk.
Its shape was printed on her sari.
Its cry rang like her anklet.
It captured his eye.
Our hero's heart stopped for a moment
and he fused with her.

śaṅke tīvraṃ bhavati samaye
śāsanaṃ Mīnaketoḥ.

labdh'|āśvāsaḥ katham api tadā
Lakṣmaṇasy' âgra|janmā
saṃdeśena praṇaya|mahatā
Maithilīṃ jīvayiṣyan,
cakre tasmai sarasija|dalaiḥ
s'|ôpacārāṃ saparyāṃ.
kānt"|āśleṣād adhika|subhagaḥ
kāminām dūta|lābhaḥ.

1.5 kṛtvā tasmin bahu|matim asau
bhūyasīm Āñjaneyād,
gāḍh'|ônmādaḥ praṇaya|padavīṃ
prāpa vārt"|ân|abhijñe.
viśleṣeṇa kṣubhita|manasāṃ
megha|śaila|drum'|ādau
yācñā|dainyaṃ bhavati—kim uta
kv' âpi saṃvedan'|ârhe.

Ved'|ôdanvad|vibhajana|vido
vaṃśa|jaṃ viśva|mūrter
āhuḥ siddhāḥ Kamalavasater
aupavāhyaṃ bhavantaṃ,
labdhaṃ yena praguṇa|gatinā
tat|priyāyāḥ sakāśāt

Fierce is the rule of Love
when he strikes at the right moment.

When he somehow breathed again,
Rama, Lákshmana's elder brother,
approached the goose with a gift
of lotus petals, hoping
to keep Sita alive with a message
of love.
Even better than a real embrace
is getting news from your lover.

A goose knows nothing of messages, yet 1.5
Rama approached him with great respect.
(Not even Hánuman received such honor.)
In his utter madness he found a way
into the bird's heart. People shaken by separation
are reduced to begging help from clouds,
mountains, trees, and so on—to say nothing
of living creatures.

Rama's Address to the Goose

You trace your lineage back
to the god of all forms, who took the form
of a goose—who could part the ocean
of the Vedas.
You carry Brahma when he leaves his lotus
for his travels. So say the seers.
And through your elegant service to his wife,
Goddess of Speech,

tat|sāvarṇyaṃ śravaṇa|rasan'|ā-
svāda|yogyā sudhā ca.

madhye ke cid vayam iha, sakhe,
kevalaṃ mānuṣāṇāṃ;
vyakt'|ôtkarṣo mahati bhuvane
vyoma|gānāṃ patis tvaṃ.
sthāne dūtyaṃ tad api bhavataḥ
saṃśrita|trāṇa|hetoḥ:
sarva|sraṣṭā Vidhir api yataḥ
sārathitvena tasthau.

icchā|mātrāj jagad aparathā
saṃvidhātuṃ kṣamāṇām
Ikṣvākūṇāṃ prakṛti|mahatām
īdṛśīṃ prekṣya velāṃ,
lakṣy'|â|lakṣye jaladhi|payasā
labdha|saṃsthāṃ Trikūṭe
Laṅkāṃ gantuṃ tava samucitaṃ
rākṣasīṃ rāja|dhānīṃ.

sthānair divyair upacita|guṇāṃ,
candan'|âraṇya|ramyāṃ,
muktā|sūtiṃ, Malaya|marutāṃ
mātaraṃ dakṣiṇ'|āśāṃ
asmat|prītyai, Janaka|tanayā|
jīvit'|ârthaṃ ca gacchann,
ekaṃ rakṣaḥ|padam iti, sakhe,
doṣa|leśaṃ sahethāḥ.

you came to be like her, adept at language
delicious to the ear.*

I, my friend, am just an ordinary man,
one among many.
You, however, are the king of birds:
your eminence is recognized world-wide.
And still it is right that you bear
my message, for I have come to you
for help. Even Brahma, the All-Creator,
once worked for Shiva as his driver.*

We Ikshvákus, born to power, were able once
to change the world at will. Look what's become of us
now. That's why you should go
to Lanka, headquarters of the demon king,
which sits astride Mount Tri·kuta in the middle of
  the ocean,
only visible at low tide.

Fly to the south.
It has plenty of fantastic temples.
Beautiful sandalwood groves.
It's the birthplace of pearls
and the mother of the Málaya breeze.
Go there and save the life of Jánaka's daughter.
Do it for me.
There's only one little thing I should mention.
It's crawling with monsters.

1.10 vācālānām iva jaḍa|dhiyāṃ
sat|*kavau* dūra|yāte,
Kailāsāya tvayi gatavati
kṣībatām āśritānāṃ,
saṃmodas te pathi pariṇamec
candrakair ujjhitānāṃ
megh'|âpāye *vipina|śikhināṃ*
vīkṣya vācaṃ|yamatvaṃ.

ā|raktānāṃ nava|madhu śanair
āpiban padminīnāṃ,
kāl'|ônnidre kuvalaya|vane
ghūrṇamānaḥ sa|līlaṃ,
svinno dānair vipina|kariṇāṃ,
saumya, seviṣyate tvām
āmodānām aham|aham|ikām
ādiśan gandha|vāhaḥ.

paryāptaṃ te pavana|calitair
aṅga|rāgaṃ parāgaiḥ
sthāne kuryuḥ sama†|samudayād
bandhavo bandhu|jīvāḥ,
yen' ânviṣyasy acala|tanayā|
pāda|lākṣ"|ânuṣaktaṃ
cūḍā|candraṃ Puravijayinaḥ
Svarṇadī|phena|pūrṇam.

1.12 *sama* HSed : *suma* HSvl

In the absence of a noble songbird, 1.10
these bird-brained peacocks never shut up.
They go mad. It happened
in the rains, when you took off for Kailása.
But clouds are history.
As you make your way south,
you'll have the utter pleasure
of seeing these peacocks, shorn of their feathers,
gone silent.*

Slowly sipping red lotus wine,
getting high in the lily beds as they open at night,
and soaked with the must of wild elephants in heat,
the wind will serve you
with a rush of odors, each vying
to be first.

It is only natural that the *bandhu·jiva* flowers
will coat your body with red pollen, borne by the wind.
True friends, they open when they see you.
You could be the crescent moon on Shiva's crest,
rounded with white water from the Ganges
falling through his hair, and stained
with lac from the time the Mountain's Daughter
angrily crowned him with her feet.*

sūkṣm'|ākārair dina|kara|karaiḥ
kalpit'|ântaḥ|śalākāḥ,
śār'|ôpāntāḥ Śatamakha|dhanuḥ|
śeṣa|citr'|âṃśukena,
ūḍhāḥ paścād ucita|gatinā
Vāyunā, rāja|haṃsa,
chatrāyeran nabhasi bhavataḥ
śāradā vāri|vāhāḥ.

drakṣyasy evaṃ, priya|sakha, sukhaṃ
laṅghit'|âdhvā sakhīṃ te:
Sītāṃ kṣetre Janaka|nṛ|pater
utthitāṃ sīra|kṛṣṭe,
gopāyantī tanum api nijāṃ
yā kathaṃ cin mad|arthaṃ
bhūmau loke vahati mahatīm
eka|patnī|samākhyāṃ

1.15 prakṣīṇāṃ tvad|viraha|samaye,
jāta|harṣām idānīṃ,
pratyāyāsyann anunaya śanaiḥ
padminīṃ svādu|vācā.
sā te tantrī|svana|subhagayā
syād it' îh' âbhyanujñāṃ,
manye, kuryān madhu|kara|girā
Maithilī|sauhṛdena.

With the thin rays of sunlight as its ribs
and bits of Indra's rainbow to dye the cloth
at its outer rim, and Wind to carry it behind you,
regal goose,
at a stately pace, the autumn clouds
will turn themselves into a royal parasol
that fills the sky.

At the end of a pleasant journey,
you, my dear friend, will see a friend:
Sita, who emerged from the furrow
her father Jánaka was plowing.*
She is barely clinging to her body, for my sake—
the true one-man woman
on earth.

Worn thin when you were away, 1.15
your partner, this lotus pond, is now happy.
Speak to her softly.
Promise you'll return
as you take leave.
I'm sure she'll give you her blessing
in the buzzing of bees, sweet
as the strumming of a string,
out of sympathy for Sita.

sārdhaṃ kāntaiḥ śabara|sudṛśām
adri|kuñjeṣu rāgād
āsīnānāṃ kṣaṇam a|samaye
dṛśya|candr'|ôdaya|śrīḥ,
uḍḍīyethāḥ sarasija|vanād
dakṣiṇ'|āś"|ânusārī,
paśyan dūrāt prabala|garutāṃ
pakṣiṇāṃ datta|vartmā.

aṅgī|kurvann amṛta|rucirām
utpatiṣṇoḥ sa|līlaṃ
chāyām antas tava maṇi|mayo
Mālyavān eṣa śailaḥ,
śobhāṃ vakṣyaty adhika|lalitāṃ
śobhamānām at' îndor
devasy' āder upajanayato
mānasād indu|bimbaṃ.

mārgau samyaṅ mama Hanumatā
varṇitau dvau. tayos te
Sahy'|āsanno 'py an|ati|subhagaḥ†
paścimo nitya|varṣaḥ.
prācīneṣu prati|jana|padaṃ
saṃhatāv adbhutānāṃ
magnā dṛṣṭiḥ katham api, sakhe,
mat|kṛte te nivāryā.

1.18 *anatisubhagaḥ* HSalt : *anaghasubhagaḥ* HSed

The Route

As you take off from the pond, savage beauties,*
lying with their lovers in rocky coves,
will briefly puzzle over the untimely rising
of the moon. Heading south,
look out for the broad-winged birds of prey
and stay out of their way.

Look: This sapphire mountain called Mályavat
will draw in your reflection,
brighter than moonlight,
like sipping the elixir of life,
as you soar past. For a moment he could be
the god of the beginning
who drew the moon out of his heart.

Hánuman has ably mapped out for me
two alternative routes. One takes you west
over the Sahya Hills. Though shorter,
it's not particularly pleasant, due to incessant rain.
The problem with the east is its endless attractions
that in place after place will dazzle your eyes.
But for my sake, friend,
you'll just have to look away.*

śrutvā śabdaṃ śravaṇa|madhuraṃ
tāvakaṃ pāmarīṇāṃ
pratyāsannāt sapadi bhavanāt
s'|ādaraṃ nirgatānām
a|bhrū|bhaṅge 'py adhika|subhagair
niścit'|âṅgaḥ kaṭ'|âkṣair
deśān etān vana|giri|nadī|
saṃvibhaktān vyatīyāḥ.

1.20 ikṣu|cchāye kisalaya|mayaṃ
talpam ātasthuṣīṇāṃ
saṃlāpais tair mudita|manasāṃ
śāli|saṃrakṣikāṇāṃ
Karṇāṭ'|Āndhra|vyatikara|vaśāt
karbure gīti|bhede
muhyantīnāṃ madana|kaluṣaṃ
maugdhyam āsvādayethāḥ.

Viṣṇor vāsād avani|vahanād
baddha|ratnaiḥ śirobhiḥ
«Śeṣaḥ sākṣād ayam,» iti janaiḥ
samyag unnīyamānaḥ,
abhrair yukto '|laghubhir a|cir'|ôn-
mukta|nirmoka|kalpair
agre bhāvī tad|anu nayane
rañjayann Añjan'|âdriḥ.

Hearing your cries, music to their ears,
country girls will rush from their homes
as you fly over their land
with its forests, mountains, rivers.
Innocent of high-brow flirting,
they'll cast sublime, sidelong glances
and see you for who you are.

In the shade of the sugar-cane, 1.20
lying on flower beds,
women who guard the paddy fields,
happily chatting about this and that,
get carried away singing songs spiced
with a mix of Kannada and Telugu.
Savor their innocence with its tinge
of mad eros.

Mount Ánjana will soon come into view,
enchanting your eyes:
Vishnu rests upon it, it holds the earth in place,
and it is crowned by precious stones.
No wonder people think it is the serpent
Shesha himself, and its ring of heavy clouds
could be the skins he's just sloughed off.*

tatr' ārūḍhair mahati manujaiḥ
svargibhiś c' âvatīrṇaiḥ
sattv'|ônmeṣād vyapagata|mithas|
tāratamy'|ādi|bhedaiḥ
sādhāraṇyāt phala|pariṇateḥ
saṃghaśo badhyamānāṃ
śaktyā kāmaṃ Madhuvijayinas
tvaṃ ca kuryāḥ saparyāṃ.

stok'|ônmagna|sphurita|pulināṃ
tvan|nivās'|êcchay" êva
drakṣyasy ārāt Kanakamukharāṃ
dakṣiṇām Añjan'|âdreḥ,
āsannānāṃ vana|viṭapināṃ
vīci|hastaiḥ prasūnāny
arcā|hetor upaharati yā
nūnam ardh'|êndu|mauleḥ.

nirviśy' âināṃ nibhṛtam an|abhi-
vyakta|mañju|praṇādo,
mand'|ādhūtaḥ pulina|pavanair
vañjul'|āmoda|garbhaiḥ,
a|vyāsaṃgaḥ sapadi padavīṃ
saṃśray' ânyair a|laṅghyo,
bandī|kuryus taṭa|vasatayo
mā bhavantaṃ kirātāḥ.

Human beings climb up this mountain
and gods climb down to it from heaven.
So intense is Vishnu's presence
that "high" and "low" disappear,
along with other such distinctions.
All reap the same reward. You, too,
can serve him with an ardent heart.
Join the crowd.

A little to the south of Mount Ánjana
you'll see the river, Rushing Gold,*
slightly lifting her skirt in the hope
that you'll nest on her shore.
With her waves she reaches out and gathers
flowers from the riverside groves,
her gift to the moon-crested god.

Enter her secretly, murmuring sweet cries,
caressed by the breeze from her shores
with its scent of scarlet flowers.
But don't get too attached.
Hit the road, where no one can reach you.
Don't get caught in the snares of the hunters
who haunt the river.

1.25 Tuṇḍīr'|ākhyaṃ tad|anu mahitaṃ
maṇḍalaṃ vīkṣamāṇaḥ
kṣetraṃ yāyāḥ kṣapita|duritaṃ
tatra Satyavrat'|ākhyaṃ,
patyau roṣāt salila|vapuṣo
yatra vāg|devatāyāḥ
setur jajñe sakala|jagatām
eka|setuḥ sa devaḥ.

nānā|ratnair upacita|guṇāṃ
nitya|saṃgīta|nādāṃ
bhūmer drakṣyasy ucita|vibhavaṃ
bhūṣaṇaṃ tatra *Kāñcīṃ*,
yasyāṃ nityaṃ nihita|nayano
Hastiśail'|âdhivāsī
dvandv'|âtītaḥ sa khalu puruṣo
dṛśyate satya|kāmaḥ.

tām āsīdan praṇama nagarīṃ
bhakti|namreṇa mūrdhnā
jātām ādau kṛta|yuga|mukhe
Dhātur icchā|vaśena,
yad|vīthīnāṃ Kari|giri|pater
vāha|veg'|âvadhūtān
dhanyān reṇūṃs tri|daśa|patayo
dhārayanty uttam'|âṅgaiḥ.

Soon you'll see ahead the splendid land of Tundíra. 1.25
Make your way to the shrine
where faults are forgiven and vows fulfilled.
It's here that the Goddess of Speech,
filled with fury at her husband,
came flooding, and God,
who alone bridges the worlds,
was the only dyke in her way.*

Woven as a brilliant web of precious stones
and other worthy strands, and always tinkling
with sweet music, the city of Kanchi
is a perfect cincture adorning
Mother Earth. Always fixed on it are the two eyes
of this Person who is beyond all twoness,
who lives on Elephant Hill,
whose passion is his truth.*

Go there, bow your head in homage
to this town that was born first,
at the onset of time,
to answer the wish of the Creator.
The highest gods roam its streets,
crowned by particles of pure dust
stirred up when the Lord of Elephant Hill
gallops past on his horse.

mand'|ādhūtāt tad|anu mahito
niḥsṛtaś cūta|ṣaṇḍāt,
pārśve tasyāḥ Paśupati|śiraś|
candra|nīhāra|vāhī,
dūrāt prāptaṃ priya|sakham iva
tvām upaiṣyaty avaśyaṃ
Kampā|pāthaḥ|kamala|vanikā|
kāmuko gandha|vāhaḥ.

varṇa|stomair iva pariṇatā
sapta|bhedair mah"|âughair,
mānyā madhye|nagaram abhitaḥ
sevitā devatābhiḥ,
svaccha|svādu|prasara|subhagā
svāminī vaḥ *kavīnāṃ*
Vegā|saṃjñāṃ vahati mahatīṃ
vallabhā Padmayoneḥ.

1.30 tīrthe puṃsāṃ śamita|kaluṣe
tatra Sārasvat'|ākhye
snātvā sārdhaṃ munibhir an|aghaiḥ,
samyag ullāsit'|âṅgaḥ,
viśvaṃ citte vigata|rajasi
vyañjayantīm a|śeṣaṃ
vakṣyasy, antar bahir api parāṃ
śuddhim a|kṣepaṇīyāṃ.

Carrying cold moonlight straight from Shiva's head
and gently brushing his mango grove
next door, the worthy breeze will surely
welcome you as a friend come from afar
before rushing on to the Kampa River
to caress its lotus clusters.

Running through the middle of the town
with seven streams like the seven
sets of sounds, and attended by gods on all sides
is the Vega River, limpid, ravishing,
Sarásvati herself, mistress of all you
fine-feathered poets.*

There, in that part of the river named for this goddess, 1.30
where people rid themselves of stains,
join the unsullied sages as they bathe.
You'll come out shining, inside and out,
and your mind, scoured and polished,
will ever after reflect all the things
of this world.

tasyās tīre Sarasijabhuvaḥ,
saumya, vaitāna|vedir
divyaṃ kurvan Draviḍa|viṣayaṃ
dṛśyate Hasti|śailaḥ,
yasy' ôpānte kṛta|vasatayo
yāpayitvā śarīraṃ
vartiṣyante vi|tamasi pade
Vāsudevasya dhanyāḥ.

saṃcinvānā taruṇa|tulasī|
dāmabhiḥ svām abhikhyāṃ,
tasyāṃ vedyām anuvidadhatī śītalaṃ†
havya|vāhaṃ,
bhog'|āiśvarya|priya|saha|caraiḥ
k" âpi Lakṣmī|kaṭ'|âkṣair
bhūyaḥ śyāmā bhuvana|jananī
devatā saṃnidhatte.

Lakṣmī|vidyul|lalita|vapuṣaṃ
tatra kāruṇya|pūrṇaṃ
mā bhaiṣīs tvaṃ marakata|śilā|
mecakaṃ vīkṣya meghaṃ.
śuddhair nityaṃ paricita|padas
tvādṛśair deva|haṃsair,
haṃsī|bhūtaḥ sa khalu bhavatām
anvavāy'|âgra|janmā.

1.32 *śītalaṃ* HSed : *śyāmalaṃ* HSalt

On its bank, my dear goose,
Elephant Hill will come into view—
Brahma's altar of creation,
which makes the whole Tamil country
a heaven on earth. Lucky are those
who live beside it: once they leave behind
their bodies, still they will stay on at Vishnu's
splendid seat.

Like a flame frozen on that altar,
with garlands of fresh basil to enrich his beauty,
and Lakshmi's jet-black eyes—
one for pleasure, one for power—
to deepen his dark sheen,
this breathtaking god who mothers the world
assumes his place.

Lakshmi, a streak of lightning, graces a body
dense with kindness and dark as emerald.
Don't be afraid if you see
a cloud, at whose feet
great seers, birds of your feather,
cluster in worship. It's a cloud
turned goose, a winged godhead,
the first-born in your line.*

sār'|āsvādī savana|haviṣāṃ
svāminas te sa devaḥ,
śuddhaṃ cakṣuḥ śruti|pariṣadāṃ,
cakṣuṣāṃ bhāga|dheyaṃ
aṅgī|kuryād vinatam amṛt'|ā-
sāra|saṃvādibhis tvām
āvir|modair abhimata|vara|
sthūla|lakṣaiḥ kaṭ'|âkṣaiḥ.

1.35 madhv|āsaktaṃ sarasi|jam iva
svinnam ālambamāno
devyā hastaṃ, tad|itara|kara|
nyasta|līl"|âravindaḥ,
devaḥ Śrīmān yadi sa viharet
svairam ārāma|bhūmau
vyakto, vāla|vyajana|vapuṣā
vījayes taṃ tvam eva.

jāta|prītir jana|padam atho
madhyamaṃ laṅghayitvā,
dūrāl lakṣya|kramuka|nivaha|
śyāmalān yāhi Colān
pratyudgacchan|makara|valana|†
stambhitaiḥ Sahyajāyāḥ
sroto|bhedair vividha|gatibhiḥ
saṃvibhakt'|âvakāśān.

1.36 *valana* HSed : *valaya* HSalt

That god savors the cream
of all your master's oblations.
He is the pure eye inside the Word
and a blessing for all eyes.
When you bow to him he'll take you in,
bathe you in his happiness,
and shower you with the exquisite bounty
of *his* eyes.

Holding one of her hands, moist like a lotus 1.35
soaked with honey, after slipping into the other
the blue lotus she likes to finger,
that god, never without Fortune,
sometimes takes the goddess for a stroll
in the temple grove. If you catch a glimpse of him,
fan him with a white flutter
of wings.

Satisfied, now, take off and cover some distance
until you come to the Chola delta.
You'll see its contours from afar:
a dark mass of areca and the Kavéri River,
a meandering web of water
changing course where schools of crocodiles
swarm upstream from the sea.

saṃdhyā|rāgaṃ surabhi|rajanī|
sambhavair aṅga|rāgaiḥ,
keśair jyotsnā|timira|kalahaṃ
pālik"|āpīḍa|garbhaiḥ
ābibhrāṇāḥ sarasija|dṛśo,
haṃsa, dol"|âdhirohād
ādhāsyante mada|kala|giras
teṣu netr'|ôtsavaṃ te.

Pṛthvī|līlā|tilaka|subhagaṃ
paścimaṃ bhāgam eṣāṃ
nāmnā Varṣaṃ, jala|cara, nadī|
mātṛkaṃ gāhamānaḥ,
drakṣyasy ārāt parimitatayā
magna|Kailāsa|dṛśyaṃ
Śvetaṃ śailaṃ, phaṇi|patim iva
kṣmā|talād ujjihānaṃ.

sphār'|āloka|praśamita|tamaḥ|
saṃcayaṃ tatra puṃsāṃ
pratyag|rūpaṃ praguṇa|vibhavaṃ
prārthanīyaṃ budhānāṃ;
nedīyāṃsaṃ kuśala|nivahaṃ
nantur ādhāsyate te
divyaṃ tejo jaladhi|tanayā|
sneha|nity'|ânuṣaktaṃ.

Bodies covered with turmeric,
like twilight come alive,
and white areca blossoms twined in their hair
as if staging the battle of moonlight and night,
the Chola girls, eyes like lotus petals,
singing softly on their swings,
are a feast for a goose's eyes.

It is as if Earth had fixed a dot
on her forehead: the land called Varsha
to the west, nourished by the river.
As soon as you fly in, water-borne bird,
you'll see White Cliff*—like a sliver
of silver Kailása, sinking into the ground,
or the giant snake from the netherworld,
stretching his brilliant hood.

For ordinary men, its wide halo dispels
the deep dark of their lives.
For the wise it is even more powerful:
it's the true self they yearn for.
As for you, if you bow there
to this luster from another world,
fed by the love of Ocean's daughter,*
it will burn endless blessings
right into your heart.

1.40 snigdha|cchāyaṃ tad|anu vitataṃ
tasya dhām' êva nīlaṃ
Nīlī|rakṣā|niyata†|lalitaṃ*
kānanaṃ saṃvicīyāḥ.
dṛṣṭe tasminn a|nimiṣa|vadhū|
nitya|nirveśa|yogye
svarg'|ôdyāna|śriyam api laghuṃ
maṃsyate mānasaṃ te.

kurvan nānā|kusuma|rajasā
yatra citraṃ vitānaṃ,
pūg'|âraṇye mṛdu vicalayan
pālikā|cāmarāṇi,
pāda|nyāsa|kṣamam avakiran
kṣmā|talaṃ puṣpa|jālaiḥ,
prāyo Vāyuḥ parijana|vidhiṃ
Pañcabāṇasya dhatte.

sroto|vegād atha jana|padaṃ,
saumya, sīmantayantī
pratyādeśo Vibudhasaritaḥ
syandate Sahya|kanyā,
kāle kāle pariṇati|vaśāt
parva|bhed'|âvakīrṇaiḥ
puṇḍr'|êkṣūṇāṃ pulina|viśadair
gadgadā mauktik'|âughaiḥ.

1.40 *rakṣāniyata* HSalt : *puṣpastabaka* HSed

As you proceed, look for a forest 1.40
where the god's black sheen
seems to blend with rich shade,
and where Indigo, the well-known monstress,
was put in charge of the charming trees.
Once you've seen it, the perfect playground
for the courtesans of the gods, your mind
will pine no more for Paradise.*

There Wind swirls a film of pollen
from many blossoms into a stunning canopy.
He gently prompts the trees in the areca grove
to whisk their white fans, and carpets
the earth with flowers to grace the feet
of the dancers. He must be second in command
in the theatre of Desire.

The Kavéri River, daughter of Sahya Mountain,
cuts through the countryside with its torrent.
It's not white sand that paves its banks
but a thick jumble of pearls that burst
from the joints of the sugar cane,* season by season,
as they turn ripe. My dear goose, from now on
you can forget about the Ganges,
that river of the gods.

Sahy'|ôtsaṅgāt sapadi Marutā
Sāgaraṃ nīyamānāṃ,
bhadr'|ālāpair vihita|kuśalāṃ
tvādṛśānāṃ *dvi|jānāṃ*,
yām a|skannāḥ sarasa|kuhalī|
patra|pātair niś"|ânte
manda|smerāṃ madhu|parimalair
vāsayant' îva pūgāḥ.

tasmin drakṣyasy amara|mahilā|
mauli|gandhair a|vandhyām,
ātanvānāṃ vyapagata|rasaṃ
Mānase mānasaṃ vaḥ,
tīrthair anyair api parigatāṃ
śuddhi|hetoḥ samantāc,
candr'|ôllāsa|prathita|yaśasaḥ
saṃpadaṃ Puṣkariṇyāḥ.

1.45 tīre tasyā viracita|padaṃ,
sādhubhiḥ sevyamānaṃ,
śraddhā|yogād vinamita|tanuḥ
Śeṣa|pīṭhaṃ bhajethāḥ,
yasminn asmat|kula|dhanatayā,
saumya, Sāketa|bhājaḥ
sthānaṃ bhāvyaṃ munibhir uditaṃ
Śrīmato Raṅgadhāmnaḥ.

Wind delivers our Kavéri from the lap
of her father, Mount Sahya, into the arms
of her bridegroom, Ocean,
while high-born birds like you
chant the mantras of blessing, and the arecas,
her closest kin, perfume her at dawn
with a shower of honeyed petals
as she ripples in a smile.*

What you see next,
when you catch a whiff
of goddesses shampooing their hair,
will quench your craving for your nesting place
in Mánasa Lake.* Water from all over
comes to bathe at Lunar Pond
ever since the moon came here for treatment
and emerged full of light.

It was installed on the bank of this lake. 1.45
It is worshiped by good people.
Make sure you go there too,
my friend,
and bow in good faith
to the Shesha Throne.
For, as the sages have predicted,
Shri Ranga·natha—now stationed in Ayódhya,
fortunately for my family—
will make his home there
one day.*

satve divye svayam udayatas
tasya dhāmnaḥ prasaṅgān,
mañjūṣāyāṃ marakatam iva
bhrājamānaṃ tad|antaḥ
ceto dhāvaty upahita|bhujaṃ,
Śeṣa|bhoge śayānaṃ,
dīrgh'|âpāṅgaṃ jaladhi|tanayā|
jīvitaṃ devam ādyaṃ.

cor'|ākrāntaṃ tad|anu vipinaṃ
Cola|Pāṇḍy'|ântara|sthaṃ
jhillī|nāda|śravaṇa|paruṣaṃ
śīghram eva vyatīyāḥ.
tīrṇe tasmin prakaṭaya, sakhe,
śītalāṃs te ninādān.
śabdāyante na khalu *kavayaḥ*
saṃnidhau dur|janānām.

srast'|āpīḍa|pracalad|alakaṃ,
vyakta|tāṭaṅka|ratnaṃ,
muktā|cūrṇa|sphurita|tilakaṃ
vaktraṃ uttānayantyaḥ
deśe tasmin kuvalaya|dṛśo
jāta|kautūhalās tvāṃ
mālā|dīrghair madhura|virutaṃ
mānayiṣyanty apāṅgaiḥ.

Speaking of that home,
a field of light pouring upward
through this heavenly site,
my heart races there to find
the long-eyed god of the beginning,
life breath of Ocean's daughter.
Still hidden like an emerald in its casket,
he will rest, one day, on that serpent's coils,
with his arm for a pillow.

But hurry on. Cross over the wild region
that separates the Chola and Pandya realms.
It's haunted by bandits and screeching crickets.*
Once it's behind you, my good friend,
you can resume your soothing song.
No real poet will open his mouth
(or beak)
for an audience of boors.

Chaplets slipping, hair askew,
so you can see the gems in their earrings
and the gleaming dots made of pearl dust
on their foreheads, ardent women
will turn their gaze upward in an instant—
weaving garlands with their lotus eyes
to honor your honeyed singing
in that country.

nity'|āvāsaṃ Vṛṣabham acalaṃ
Sundar'|ākhyasya Viṣṇoḥ
pratyāsīdan sapadi vinato†
bhāga|dheyaṃ nataḥ syāḥ,
yasy' ôtsaṅge Bali|vijayinas
tasya mañjīra|vāntaṃ
pātho divyaṃ Paśupati|jaṭā|
sparśa|hīnaṃ vibhāti.

1.50 Īśād astrāṇy adhigatavatāṃ
kṣatriyāṇāṃ prabhāvāt
kārā|vāsa|smaraṇa|cakitaiḥ
sikta|sasyān payo|daiḥ
paśyan yāyāḥ param Alakayā
spardhamānair a|jasraṃ
puṇy'|āvāsaiḥ pura|janapadair
maṇḍitān Pāṇḍya|deśān.

muktā|jālair janita|pulināṃ
śukti|saṃtāna|muktais,
tārā|pūrṇaṃ divam iva, tatas
Tāmraparṇīṃ bhajethāḥ,
pratyāsattyā niyata|viśadaṃ
pīta|sindhor maharṣeḥ.
pānīyaṃ te pariṇamayitā
tatra *mukt'/āmayatvaṃ*.

1.49 *vinato* HSed : *vinamad°* HSv

Soon you'll arrive at Bull Mountain.
Here Vishnu, "The Beautiful," is always at home.
Here the humble find fortune.
Humble yourself.
When God stretched his foot high,
his anklet set free the heavenly river
that fell straight into the lap
of this shining mountain, shunning
Shiva's tangled hair.*

Trembling at the memory of their term 1.50
in the prison of the Madurai kings,
who were armed by Shiva himself, clouds
never fail to water these fields.
Take a good look at the Pandya land,
its villages and towns teeming with temples,
by far superior to Álaka (that northern city
Kali·dasa adored.)*

Don't miss the Tamra·parni River,
her sands formed of pearls released
by zillions of oysters, like a sky
glowing with stars. She is always crystal-clear
thanks to Agástya, who lives nearby—
the sage who drank the ocean dry.
Even you will turn pure
as a pearl, released in her water,
the ultimate cure.*

tasyāḥ svairaṃ sarasija|mukh'|ā-
svāda|saṃprīta|cetāḥ,
śītī|bhūtas tarala|laharī|
bāhu|saṃśleṣaṇena,
adhyāsīnaḥ pulinam, anilair
vījitaś Candan'|âdreḥ,
śrāntiṃ śāntiṃ gamayatu bhavān
sāgaraṃ laṅghayiṣyan.

savyaṃ tasyāḥ kiyad iva gataḥ,
śyāma|tālī|tamālāṃ,
tvat|prāyāṇāṃ taruṇa|vayasāṃ
cetaso nandayitrīṃ
velām abdher vividha|laharī|
datta|mukt"|âbhirāmāṃ
drakṣyasy ārād dvi|guṇa|pulināṃ
ketakīnāṃ parāgaiḥ.

sthitvā tatra kṣaṇam, ubhayataḥ
śaila|śṛṅg'|âvatīrṇaiḥ
sroto|bhedair adhigata|guṇaṃ
cāru|viṣphāra|ghoṣaiḥ,
lakṣyī|kurvan Daśamukha|purīṃ,
saumya, patra|prakṛṣṭo,
velā|cāpaṃ śara iva, sakhe,
vegatas tvaṃ vyatīyāḥ.

Savor the lips of her lotus petals
to your heart's delight. Let her embrace you
with her tremulous, cool waves. Take your time.
Sit awhile on her banks, while the winds
from the Sandal Mountain massage you.
You're about to cross the ocean.
Put your toils to rest.

Veer slightly to the left and soon
you'll see the ocean shore, dotted
with dark *tamála* trees and with palmyra palms,
brushed white with pearls offered by the waves,
its sands silvered by pandanus pollen.
A favorite haunt for young love-birds,
like you.

There, my dear dear friend, two split streams
pouring down from both flanks of the mountain
supply the shore, curved as a bow,
with its string and the pleasant twang
of their torrent. Standing on the peak,
aim yourself at the city of the ten-headed demon,
and let go—like a well-feathered arrow.

1.55 dāv'|āsaktaṃ vanam iva, nabhaḥ
saṃdhyay" êv' ânuviddhaṃ,
sindūr'|âṅkaṃ dvi|pam iva, Hariṃ
sv'|âmbareṇ' êva juṣṭaṃ,
vidyud|bhinnaṃ ghanam iva, sakhe,
vidrum'|âraṇya|yogād
dehen' âikaṃ mithunam iva ca
drakṣyasi tvaṃ payo|dhiṃ.

asmat|pūrvaiḥ Surapati|hṛtaṃ
draṣṭu|kāmais turaṅgaṃ
bhittvā kṣoṇīm a|gaṇita|balaiḥ
sāgaro vardhit'|ātmā
sat|kār'|ârthaṃ tava yadi girīn
ādiśed gupta|pakṣān,
a|śrānto 'pi praṇayam ucitaṃ
n' âiva bandhor vihanyāḥ.

tatr' āsīnaḥ kva cana sarasi
smera|hem'|âravinde,
labdh'|āsvādo madhubhir a|mitaiḥ,
saṃvinīt'|âdhva|khedaḥ,
drakṣyasy agre laghutara|gatiḥ
śeṣam ullaṅghya sindhos
toy'|āghātān masṛṇita|śilā|
ramya|velaṃ Suvelaṃ.

Like a forest aflame, like the sky shot through 1.55
with twilight, an elephant in procession, splattered
with red, like dark blue Vishnu
in his saffron suit, or a rain cloud
pierced by lightning, you'll see beneath you,
my friend, the sea and its coral reef,
two bodies become one.

When former kings in my line sought the steed
that Indra stole, they dug, en masse, a deep
hole in the earth, extending Ocean's domain.
If he were now to order his submarine mountains,
the few whose wings are still intact, to emerge
and welcome a guest, don't reject
this friendly gesture, whether weary
or not.*

After resting there in some lake, its golden
lotuses all smiles, and refreshing yourself
from the journey by feasting on their sap,
cross what's left of the ocean, feeling lighter.
Ahead you'll see Mount Goodshore,
cliffs shorn smooth by pounding waves
along its stunning coast.

yasy' āsanne payasi jala|dhes
tvat|praticchanda|candrāḥ,
pakṣa|ccheda|kṣarita|rudhira|
stoma|saṃdarśanīyāḥ,
vīci|prāpter viṣamita|ruco
mauktikais tārak'|ābhaiḥ
saṃdhyām anyāṃ niyatam
avanau darśayanti pravālāḥ;

yatr' âraṇyaṃ Varuṇa|vasater
vīci|veg'|âpanītair
muktā|ratna|stabaka|śabalair
vidrumair utpravālaṃ,
rakṣo|bhītaiḥ svayam a|nimiṣair
āhṛta|sthāpitānāṃ
mandārāṇāṃ madhu|parimalair
vāsitaṃ mauli|daghnaiḥ;

1.60 tasmin dṛśyā bhavati† bhavataś
cāru|saudh'|âvadātā
Laṅkā sindhor mahita|puline
rāja|haṃs" îva līnā,
tvām āyāntaṃ pavana|taralair
yā patāk'|âpadeśaiḥ
pakṣair abhyujjigamiṣur iva
sthāsyati śrāvya|nādā.

1.60 *bhavati* HSed : *tadanu* HSalt

Red as the blood the mountains shed when Indra
chopped off their wings, shimmering at each touch
of the waves, ocean pearls for stars and your reflection
for the moon, the coral reefs offshore
forever bring another twilight
down to earth.*

And there's a grove there, unfolding its coral buds
and clusters of gems and pearl grafted
by Ocean's hurried waves—immersed,
top to bottom, in the fragrant juices of the wishing trees
hauled away from heaven and transplanted,
without blinking an eye, by the gods themselves,
in their dread of the Demon.

There, nesting in the splendid sand, Lanka, 1.60
washed white with palaces, will reveal herself
just to you, like a queenly goose. You'll hear
her beckoning call. With streamers flapping
in the wind, she'll be whirling her wings
as she rises up to welcome you
on arrival.

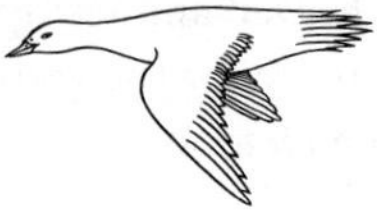

SECOND PART

2.1 LĪLĀ|KHELAṂ lalita|gamanāś,
cāru|nādaṃ sa|śiñjāḥ,
bhall'|âkṣaṃ tvāṃ Smara|śara|dṛśo,
gauram ā|pāṇḍur'|âṅgyaḥ,
mugdh'|ālāpaṃ madhura|vacaso,
Mānas'|ârhaṃ mano|jñāḥ
yatr' ānītāḥ sura|yuvatayo
rañjayeyuḥ samakṣam;

agraiḥ śāpair upahati|bhiyā
rakṣasā dūra|muktāḥ,
dagdhuṃ yogyā Hutavaham api,
tvat|priyā|varṇa|śuddhāḥ,
utpaśyantyo Janaka|tanayā|
tejas" âiva sva|rakṣāṃ
rodhaṃ yasyām anuvidadhate
loka|pāl'|âvarodhāḥ;

adhyāsīnā bahu|maṇi|mayaṃ
tuṅga|śṛṅgaṃ Suvelaṃ,
dik|pāleṣu prathita|yaśasā
rakṣasā rakṣyamāṇā,
agre Meror a|mara|nagarīṃ
yā pariṣkāra|bhūmnā
tv āhūy' êva dhvaja|paṭa|mayān
agra|hastān dhunoti;

THERE YOU'LL come face to face 2.1
with goddesses, kidnapped and held hostage:
Their playful gaits will match your graceful play,
the tinkling of their anklets, your charming call,
their gaze (the flowering arrows
of Love), your darting eyes,
their ivory limbs, white sheen of wings,
sweet tongues, your gentle whisper,
their raids on the heart, your Heart Lake* home.
They'll flirt with you,
geese to a gander.

The Demon brought them here, but won't touch them.
A curse decrees that he'll die if he does.
White as your loving mate, and quite capable
of burning up Fire himself, the wives of the gods
who guard the four directions spend their days
in prison. They pin their hopes for release
on the flame that smolders
inside Jánaka's daughter.

Poised on the jewel-studded peak of Mount Goodshore,
and well guarded by that Demon whose fame
is sung by the four guardians of the compass,
this city, decked with gold, brandishes
her banners as if poking fingers in the face
of her rival, the city of the gods,
on the roof of the world.

kāle yasyāṃ vyapagata|ghane
tvad|vihār'|ôcite 'smin
candr'|ālokair vilulita|dhiyāṃ
Śarvarī|garva|hāsaiḥ
svarga|strīṇāṃ viraha|janitaṃ
bāṣpam udvelayantyo
niḥṣyandante salila|kaṇikāś
candra|kānta|sthalīnāṃ;

2.5 bhāsā tādṛk|pariṇati|juṣā
Maithilī|śoka|vahner
bhasmī|bhūtāṃ Pavanatanaya|
snehinā Pāvakena,
antas|trāsād avahita|dhiyaḥ
saṃvidhāsyanty avaśyaṃ
pratyādiṣṭa|prathama|racanaṃ
Viśvakarm'|ādayas tāṃ.

madhye tasyā niśi|cara|pateḥ
sadma ruddh'|ântarikṣaṃ
yugmaṃ neyair divi su|manasāṃ
sevyamānaṃ vimānaiḥ.
kār"|āgāraṃ vibudha|sudṛśāṃ
vīkṣamāṇo vicitraṃ
śoka|prīti|vyatikaravatīṃ
vakṣyase citta|vṛttiṃ.

The clouds are no longer there
to spoil your fun, and Lady Night is laughing
with her lunar lover whose bright beams
unnerve the captive women from heaven,
sobbing in solitude and frustration,
and their tears well up and overflow
when moon-rays melt the moonstones
that pave the palace floors.

Only yesterday this city was burnt to ashes 2.5
by Fire, riding the tail of Hánuman,
son of the Wind—a fire fed by Sita's
scorching grief. But by the time you fly in,
I'm sure they'll have it rebuilt. Vishva·karman*
and his crew from heaven, terror in their hearts,
will outdo their own earlier
architectural wonder.

At the center of town, you'll see
the palace of the demon king, so high
that it dominates the sky.
Outside are parked his fancy
double-seated private jets,
stolen from the gods.
Nearby is the splendid prison
where the women of heaven are inmates.
Don't be surprised if you feel confused
by a mixture of sorrow and fascination.

īṣat|kopāc cakita|pavanām,
indu|saṃdigdha|sūryāṃ,
nity'|ôdārām ṛtubhir a|khilair
niṣkuṭe vṛkṣa|vāṭīṃ
Sītā|śoka|jvalana|saha|jais
tatra dīptām aśokair
āpadyethāḥ prathama|lulitām
Āñjaneya|pracāraiḥ.

tasyām anyair viyati viha|gaiḥ
sārdham ānanda|nighnaiḥ
sthāne sthāne nihita|nayano
vartayan maṇḍalāni,
drakṣyasy ekāṃ Janaka|duhituḥ,
saumya, dur|jāta|bandhuṃ
nyast'|ākalpāṃ kva cana viṭape
śiṃśupāṃ sāndra|śākhāṃ.

mūle tasyāḥ kim api savana|
kṣetra|saṃskāra|jātaṃ,
yatra kv' âpi sthitam api, sakhe,
trāsa|hīnaṃ mahimnā,
kāle tasmin katham api mayā
vīrya|śulkena labdhaṃ
dṛśyaṃ tat te dina|kara|kula|
dyotakaṃ divya|ratnaṃ.

At the slightest sign of his displeasure,
the wind is startled and dies down, the fierce sun
passes for the moon, and all six seasons work
round the clock, tending the trees
in his garden. Approach that grove,
ablaze with red *ashóka* blossoms, burning with
Sita's sorrow. Notice the twisted branches,
remnants of Hánuman's recent frenzy.

Circle overhead together with all the other
happy birds. Scan each and every corner
until you see one lush tree, Sita's sole friend
in disaster. Somewhere, my dear goose,
on one of its branches, she's hidden
her last possession.

At the foot of that tree there is something
for you to see—mined from a furrow
in a field that was cleared for offering,
free of fear or flaw, no matter where, and ever glowing,
the brightest jewel of heaven that lights up
the heirs of the sun, someone I somehow
won, at the time, and wed, putting my courage
at stake.*

2.10 sā me dṛṣṭiḥ, śaphara|nayanā,
samnata|bhrūḥ, su|keśī,
tanvī, tuṅga|stana|bhara|natā,
tapta|jāmbūnad'|ābhā
bālā yuṣmat|pratima|gamanā,
vedi|madhyā, var'|âṅgī,
śṛṅgār'|ākhyaṃ nidhim adhigatā
śreyasī devat" êva.

sā te yāvan nayana|padavīṃ
yāti moh'|âlasā vā,
saṃdeśaṃ vā mad|upagataye
śrāvayantī śakuntān,
aty|āsanna|priya|vacanatāṃ
sūcayadbhir nimittair
etām aśru|sthagita|nayanaṃ
vīkṣamāṇā diśaṃ vā,
ākalpān vā savidha|nihitān
ālapantī vimohād,
«aṅga|sparśo Raghu|kula|pateḥ
smaryate vā na v"?» êti,
dhyāyantī vā cira|virahitān
eka|śayyā|vihārān.
tasyā nūnaṃ niyati|janitā
tādṛśī kāla|yātrā.

She's the apple of my eye. Her eyes are two black fish 2.10
under finely arched brows and jet-dark hair.
So thin she is
she staggers slightly under the burden of her breasts.
Her skin of molten gold, her youth, her gait—
so like yours—
her hourglass waist: this perfect woman,
like the highest goddess, stole the treasury
of infinite charm.

Finally she will come into focus, possessed, perhaps,
by delusion. Maybe she's cross-examining the birds
for news
of my arrival, or scanning the horizon, her eyes veiled
by tears, for signs that some word from her lover
is imminent. She might even be conversing
with her ornaments, hidden somewhere nearby:
"Do you or do you not remember what it feels like
to be touched by Rama?"
Or she could be absorbed in the joys
of lying together, in a single bed, though they are now
long past. Fate has reduced her, I'm sure, to these ways
of killing time.

śuddhām indoḥ śva|paca|bhavane
kaumudīṃ visphurantīm,
ānītāṃ vā viṣa|taru|vane
Pārijātasya śākhāṃ,
s'|ûktiṃ ramyāṃ khala|parisare
sat|kaveḥ kīrtyamānāṃ
manye dīnāṃ niśi|cara|gṛhe
Maithilasy' ātma|jātāṃ,

varṣ'|ākīrṇām iva kamalinīṃ,
vyāhat'|ârthām iv' ôktiṃ,
paṅk'|āśliṣṭām iva bisa|latāṃ,
paty|apetām iv' êbhīṃ,
megha|cchannām iva śaśi|kalāṃ,
vighna|ruddhām iv' āśāṃ,
vyāghr'|ôpetām iva mṛga†|vadhūṃ,
bhū|tale jyām iv' āstāṃ,

2.15 smṛtvā pūrvaṃ Smara|śara|bhaye
mat|pariṣvaṅga|rakṣām
āśliṣyantīm a|lasa|valitair
aṅgakair mātaraṃ svāṃ,
ākalpe 'pi śramam adhigatair
aṅga|rāge 'pi khinnair
a|kṣāmyadbhiḥ smṛtim api muhuḥ
saukumāry'|âtirekāt,

2.14 *mṛga* HSed : *śaśa* HSvl

Like a burst of pure moonlight
in the dog-eater's hut,
or a white shoot of the paradise tree
planted in poison ivy,
like a lyrical line by a real poet
sung to a mean-hearted crowd—
that's how I think of the girl from Míthila,
miserable captive of the demon
who haunts the night,

like a cluster of lotuses scattered by heavy rain,
like a sentence that has lost its meaning,
a lotus stem lying in the mud,
a she-elephant robbed of her mate,
the crescent moon swallowed by clouds,
like hope impeded, or a doe within reach of a tiger,
like a string torn from the bow, left behind
on the field of battle.

She's remembering how I used to protect her from 2.15
the deadly arrows of Desire,
whose other name is Memory, by holding her tight,
too weary even to bear the weight of a single adornment,
or of soothing powders, or even the burden of her
memories,
her fragile body failing, clinging now to her mother,
Earth,

bhūyo bhūyaḥ kara|sarasije
nyasya rom'|âñcit'|âṅgīṃ,
maulau cūḍā|maṇi|virahite
nirviśantīṃ nidhāya,
antas|tāpād adhigata|rujor
ādarād arpayantīṃ
paryāyeṇa stana|kalaśayor
aṅgulīyaṃ madīyaṃ,

ambā|tulyā su|carita|phalaṃ
divyam ālepanaṃ prāg
aṅgeṣv asyāḥ sthiram anuguṇaṃ
yad vitene 'nasūyā,
dhār"|ākāraiḥ stana|kalaśayor
āpatadbhiḥ samantāt
saṃtāp'|ôṣṇais tad|anu bahulair
aśrubhiḥ kṣālayantīṃ,

a|grāhyatvād viṣama|yamitaṃ
keśa|hastaṃ mayā prāg
ābibhrāṇāṃ tanu|parimala|
śraddhay" êv' âvakīrṇaṃ,
arcā|hetor bhuvi Rati|pater
apsarobhir vimuktām
anvag|yātām iva sura|taror
mañjarīṃ cañcarīkaiḥ,

passing the ring I sent her from hand to hand, each time
with a rush of pleasure, then rolling it through her
crownless hair
in ecstasy, and from there down to her burning breasts,
each one in turn, sick with yearning.

And that magic, long-lasting lotion that once
the hermit's wife, Anasúya, gave her
as a reward, rubbing it all over her perfect body
with a mother's care—she's washing it away
with searing torrents of tears that shatter against
the round rims of her breasts,*

and that cascading hair, that once I tried to braid
and failed, so that the strands came out uneven—
now it's disheveled, as if each lock were trying to absorb
another bodily fragrance, or as if the dancing girls
in heaven
had cast down to earth a spray from the wishing tree,
swarming with black bees, a gift
to the deity of desire.

ānītaṃ yat tvaritam a|calād
uttarīyaṃ plavaṅgair
asy' ākāraiḥ sadṛśam abhitas
tvat|priyā|rūpa|cihnaṃ,
bāl'|āditya|dyuti|saha|caraṃ
cāru|vāso vasānāṃ,
saṃdhyā|rāga|vyatikaravatīṃ
candra|lekhām iv' ânyāṃ,

2.20 vaktuṃ mārgaṃ kila vasumatīṃ
jagmuṣas tat|pad'|âbjāt
mañjīrasya tvad|upama|ruter
dakṣiṇasy' âsya tulyaṃ,
aṅk'|ārūḍhe caraṇa|kamale
mat|kareṇ' ôpadheyaṃ,
vāmaṃ śākhā|śikhara|nihitaṃ
vīkṣya gāḍhaṃ viṣaṇṇāṃ,

aṅgair mlāyat|kisalaya|samair
ujjhit'|ākalpa|puṣpair,
gāḍh'|āśliṣṭāṃ vapuṣi vi|male
bimbitābhir latābhiḥ,
saṃtāp'|ôṣṇa|śvasana|paruṣa|
cchāyayā kiṃ cid ūnāṃ,
bandī|bhūtāṃ niśi|cara|gṛhe
Nandanasy' êva lakṣmīṃ,

Look at this wisp of her scarf, which the monkeys
found in the mountains and brought to me: it has a row
of geese
modeled on your mate and the color of the rising sun.
She'll be wearing its matching sari, my favorite pattern,
like a sliver of the moon wrapped in red twilight.

And this right anklet of hers— 2.20
the one that rings like your voice—
walked away from her foot
and came down to earth as if to show me
the way. Its twin—the one that I
should be tying to her lotus foot
when it comes to rest on my lap—
is hidden high in a branch above her.
I'm sure that whenever she looks at it,
her heart sinks.*

What would happen to the lush trees of heaven
if they were scorched by a hot desert wind?
No wonder that she's not quite herself, locked up
by that monster who haunts the night. Her arms,
shoots withering on the branch, are shorn of
the blossoms
she would normally wear, and she's held tight
by the vines
that mirror her slender frame, her beauty parched
by feverish sighs.

ceto|vṛttiṃ śamayati bahiḥ
sārvabhaume nirodhe
mayy ekasmin praṇihita|dhiyaṃ
Mānmathen' āgamena,
abhyasyantīm an|itara|juṣo
bhāvanāyāḥ prakarṣāt
sv'|ânten' ântar|vilaya|mṛdunā
nir|vikalpaṃ samādhiṃ,

śūnyā dṛṣṭiḥ, śvasitam adhikaṃ,
mīlitaṃ vaktra|padmaṃ,
dhār"|ākāraṃ nayana|salilaṃ,
s'|ânubandho vilāpaḥ—
itthaṃ dainyaṃ kim api vidhinā
dur|nivāreṇa nītā
sā me saktā† tanutara|tanus
tapyate nūnam antaḥ.

dṛṣṭvā tasyās tvam api karuṇāṃ
tādṛśīṃ tām avasthāṃ,
śakṣyasy antaḥ svayam upanataṃ
śoka|vegaṃ na soḍhuṃ.
kravy'|âdānāṃ Daśavadanavat
kv' âpi jātāv a|jātāḥ
n' ālambante katham iva dayāṃ
nirmalatv'|ôpapannāḥ.

2.23 *saktā* HSed : *sītā* HSalt

I'm sure she's practicing Yoga—
calming the mind by blocking everything external,
focusing her awareness entirely on one thing:
me. The text she follows
is the Scripture of Love. In the vast power
of her imagination, which has no other
object, her heart melting,
she's dissolving into
the deepest place.

An empty gaze, sigh upon sigh, a face fading
away, a rising tide of tears, incessant lament—
what unutterable misery has been forced on her
by fate! And still, all skin and bones,
consumed from inside,
she sticks fast to me.

Seeing her in that heartbreaking state, you too
will not be able to hold back a surge of sorrow
swelling up in your pure heart. It would take a ten-faced
Rávana, who feeds on flesh, not to feel
a pinch of pity.

2.25 nedīyasyām adhigata|raso
dīrghikāyāṃ nikāmaṃ,
saṃveśena śramam apanayan
śarvarīṃ yāpayethāḥ,
itthaṃ nidrā|samayam ucitaṃ
vīkṣya naktaṃ|carīṇāṃ,
pratyūṣe tvaṃ praṇaya|madhurāṃ
śrāvayiṣyan mad|uktiṃ.

śītair adhva|śrama|vinayanaiḥ
sevito gandha|vāhaiḥ,
suptaḥ svairaṃ pulina|śayane
sv|antare candra|pādaiḥ,
krīḍā|gītaiḥ kamala|mukule
līyatāṃ† ṣaṭ|padānāṃ
kāry'|ākāṅkṣī kalayatu bhavān,
rāja|haṃsa, prabodhaṃ.

tām ārūḍhaś cala|kisalayāṃ
śiṃśupāṃ sv'|âika|lakṣyo,
mandī|kurvan Manasija|dhanur|
ghoṣa|tīvraṃ ninādaṃ,
mohād īṣan|muṣita|manasaṃ
bodhaya preyasīṃ me,
ramyām ādau Raghu|Janakayor
varṇayan vaṃśa|kīrtiṃ:

2.26 *līyatāṃ* HSed : *pīyatāṃ* HSvl : *dīyatāṃ* HSalt

Right next to her is a pool where you can finally drink 2.25
and rest to your heart's delight. Spend the night there
and recover your strength, preparing to speak my
loving words
at dawn, when the monstresses who thrive in darkness
fall asleep.

A cool, kind breeze will guard you as you sleep
on a bed of sand, soft with moonlight. Refreshed
and eager to fulfill your mission, O honorable gander,
you'll wake to the happy hum of bees, sealed
in the honey trap of the lotus, not yet open.

Perch yourself on a swaying branch of that
shínshupa tree,
where only one person can see you. Tone down your
honking,
haunting as the twang of the bow of Desire
who lurks in the heart. You can begin by singing
the sunny story of the Raghu and Jánaka clans,
to wake up my loved one—for dejection
is steadily eating away
at her heart:

«patyur, devi, praṇaya|sacivaṃ
viddhi dīrgh'|āyuṣo māṃ
jīvātuṃ te dadhatam an|aghaṃ
tasya saṃdeśam antaḥ,
śūrāṇāṃ yaḥ śarad|upagame
vīra|patnī|varāṇāṃ
saṃmān'|ârhaṃ samayam ucitaṃ
sūcayet kūjitaiḥ svaiḥ.»

mat|prastāva|pravaṇam atha sā
Maithilī mānayet tvāṃ,
mlānaṃ śokād vadana|kamalaṃ
mandam unnamya bhīruḥ,
antas|toṣād amṛta|laharī|
labdha|sa|brahmacaryair
ambho|jānām uṣasi miṣatām
antar|aṅgair apāṅgaiḥ.

2.30 paśyantī sā Raghu|pati|vadhūs
tvām a|śeṣ'|âvadātaṃ,
pratyāśvāsād adhigata|ruciḥ,
prāktan" îv' êndu|lekhā,
mat|saṃdeśe tad|anu su|mukhī
s'|âvadhānā bhavitrī.
kiṃ na strīṇāṃ janayati mudaṃ
kānta|vārt"|āgamo 'pi.

"Allow me, lady, to introduce myself:
I am a trusted friend of your husband—
long may he live! I have within me a life-saving
cure, a message he sends to you. I'm the one
who cries out at the onset of autumn,
who rallies soldiers, husbands of brave women,
to seize the moment."*

As she hears your well-chosen words
about me, that timid girl from Míthila will honor you
with rapt attention, lifting up, just a little,
a face withered by sorrow. Deep happiness,
like sweet nectar, will surge up from inside
to the corners of her eyes, two buds
unfolding at dawn.

Once she sees you, whiter than white, 2.30
she'll take heart and take on color
like the crescent moon reemerging
from darkness. Then our Raghu princess
will be fully awake and ready for my message.
Elation erupts in a woman when word comes
from her lover.

paścād evaṃ kathaya, «bhavatī|
bhāga|dheyena jīvan
kalyāṇīṃ tvāṃ kuśalam an|aghaḥ
Kosal'|êndro 'nuyuṅkte,
yeṣu śreyo bhavati niyataṃ,
tāni sarvāṇi santo
Lakṣmyā devyās tava ca bhuvane
lakṣaṇāny āmananti.

yasyā yasmin vyavadhir abhavad
bhūṣaṇ'|ālepan'|ādir,
nītām enāṃ† niyati|vibhavād
antarīpaṃ davīyaḥ,
pratyāsīdann iva nayanayor
vartmani sthāpayitvā
sa tvām evaṃ vadati kuśalī,
devi, sakhyā mukhena.

‹vel"|âtīta|praṇaya|vivaśaṃ
bhāvam āseduṣor nau
bhog'|ārambhe kṣaṇam iva gatā
pūrvam āliṅgan'|ādyaiḥ;
saṃpraty eṣā, su|tanu, śataśaḥ
kalpanā|saṃgamais taiś
cintā|dīrghair api śakalitā†
śarvarī n' âpayāti.

2.32 *enāṃ* HSed : *evaṃ* HSvl 2.33 *api śakalitā* HSalt : *aviśakalitā* HSed

Start off like this: "The flawless King of Kósala,
who's kept alive by your blessing, prays that all is well
with you. The very essence of felicity in this world,
so say the wise, exists solely in the Goddess of Fortune
and in you.

Once he and you would not allow even a necklace,
even a fine powder, to come between you.
Now you've been exiled by fate to an island
at the end of the world. But he's here, as it were,
and as if he could see you with his own eyes he's
happily talking with you, using a friend
for a mouth.

The Message

'The two of us had reached the point
where we would lose ourselves in a tenderness
without limit. A whole night passed like a second
from the moment we started to make love—
the first hug and all that follows. That was then.
And now, lovely girl, that same night, shattered
into pieces by countless images of loving
and too many thoughts, never ends.*

uddāmais te kuca|kalaśayor
ūṣmabhir nirjitena,
chidraṃ labdhvā viraha|samaye
tat|kṣaṇād unnatena
kund'|āmodaiḥ surabhita|diśā
gandha|vāhena dainyaṃ
saṃprāpto 'haṃ, saha sarasi|jais
tvan|mukh'|âmbhoja|mitraiḥ.

2.35 mādhvī|digdhair virahi|vanitā|
svāda|lubdhair a|moghair
āvṛṇvantaṃ Kusumadhanuṣaś
citra|puṅkhair dig|antān,
«Sītā|pārśve na bhavatu bhavān,»
ity avocad Vasantaṃ
Rāmas trāsād a|namita|dhanur
maulinā saṃnatena.

pārśve lolaiḥ parabhṛta|kulair
mukta|kolāhalānāṃ,
mallī|reṇu|sthagita|vapuṣāṃ,
mandaraṃ nirgatānāṃ,
bhīten' âhaṃ bhramara|paṭalī|
śṛṅkhalā|saṃkulānāṃ
mārge tiṣṭhan Malaya|marutāṃ
vārito Lakṣmaṇena.

Defeated, in those days, by the heat welling up
from your breasts, the cold wind has now seized
this moment
of our separation. Wasting no time, he blasts
the fragrance of jasmine to the farthest corners of space
and reduces me, together with the lotus petals,
so like your face,
to misery.

And as for Spring, who fills up space with the unerring 2.35
flower-arrows of Desire, dripping with honey,
with rainbow
feathers, thirsty for the lives of lonely women—
I, Rama, begged him in terror, bowing my head,
my bow
undrawn: "Please, Sir, keep far away
from Sita."

The Southern Wind, flanked on both sides
by hordes of cuckoos crying out in ecstasy,
and heavily armed with iron chains made of swarming
black bees, marching slowly, coated
with jasmine dust, was advancing
against me, but at the last minute Lákshmana,
terrified, rushed to my rescue.

mando vakṣye kim iva Janakaṃ?
kiṃ nu yog'|īśvaro mām?
ity evaṃ me, su|tanu, manaso
vartayanti sma khedaṃ
rakt'|âśoke jvalati sa|vidhe
lāja|varṣ'|âbhirāmaiḥ
puṣp'|âughais tvat|pariṇaya|daśāṃ
vyañjayantaḥ karañjāḥ.

ceto n' âiva tyajati capalā|
hema|koṇ'|âbhighātād
dhīr'|ôdātta†|stanita|jaladāt
tāṇḍav'|ārambham icchan,
vāt'|ônmuktaiḥ kuṭaja|kusumair
vāsite śaila|śṛṅge
rakṣaḥ|pīḍā|rahita|dayit"|ā-
śleṣa|dhanyo mayūraḥ.

śaila|vyakta|prati|vilapitāṃ,
sāndra|tāp'|ânuviddhāṃ
tanvānānāṃ nayana|salilair
mātaraṃ te sa|bāṣpāṃ,
paśyantīnāṃ prabala|madan'|ôn-
māda|paryākulaṃ māṃ,
prāyo jātaṃ kim api ruditaṃ
vyomni kādambinīnām.

2.38 *udātta* HSed : *udāra* HSvl

Fool that I am, what can I say to Jánaka,
and what will that wise old man say to me?
Such bitter questions, my dear, keep whirling
through my mind when I see white *karánja* blossoms
raining down on the red *ashóka*, aflame nearby,
like the showering of parched rice as you took my hand
and we circled the wedding fire.*

This frenzied peacock has taken hold of my mind:
itching to start his dance to the deep rumbling
of thunder, when lightning strikes like a golden
drumstick and the mountain peaks are redolent
of wild jasmine scattered by the wind. I envy his
happy embrace by his mate, with no demon
to prey upon them.

In her rumbling mountain coves, the earth,
your mother, echoes the lament of an advancing
storm, and teardrops falling from the sky make her weep,
too, as steam hisses from her scorched body.
And when that wall of clouds sees me, swept away
in mad torrents of feeling, the whole world is convulsed
in wailing.

2.40 deha|sparśaṃ Malaya|pavane,
drṣṭi|saṃbhedam indau,
dhām'|âikatvaṃ jagati, bhuvi c' â|
bhinna|paryaṅka|yogaṃ,
tārā|citre viyati vitatiṃ
śrī|vitānasya paśyan—
dūrī|bhūtāṃ, su|tanu, vidhinā
tvām ahaṃ nirviśāmi.

prāptaiḥ sakhyaṃ tava nayanayoḥ
padma|kośaiḥ prabuddhaiḥ
saṃnāhaṃ naḥ samaya|niyataṃ
sādhu saṃdhukṣayantī,
senā|yogyāṃ saraṇim adhunā
darśayantī śubh'|āśā,
Sīte, nūnaṃ tvarayati śarat
tvat|samīpaṃ ninīṣuḥ.

tāt'|ādeśāt sapadi Bharate
nyasta|rājy'|âbhiṣekaṃ
yā mām ekā vanam anugatā
rāja|dhānīṃ vihāya,
tām eva tvām ucita|śayanāṃ
bāhu|madhye madīye
dūre kṛtvā† guṇavati muhur
dūyate jīvitaṃ me.

2.42 *kṛtvā* HSed : *kartur* HSalt

Our bodies touch 2.40
in the southern wind.
Our eyes meet
in the moon.
We live together in a single home—
the world, and the earth
is the one bed we share.
The sky scattered with stars
is a canopy stretched above us.
Think of this, my lean beauty:
however far away
fate has taken you from me,
I still find my way
into you.

As the lotus buds, twins to your eyes, awake,
Autumn hastens our final preparations,
for the moment is ripe and the way is clear
for our march under cloudless skies. Sita:
Time itself is in a hurry, eager
to lead me to you.

When in an instant, at Father's command, I handed
the kingdom to Bharata and set out for the wilderness,
you, only you, followed me, leaving the city behind.
It's the harrowing story of my life that you,
my loyal wife, are so far away
when you should be resting
in my arms.*

setuṃ baddhvā vipulam a|calaiḥ
sāyakair vā payo|dhau,
kṛtvā Laṅkāṃ srajam iva kare
khelatāṃ vānarāṇāṃ,
alpīyobhiḥ, su|mukhi, divasair
yodhayan yātu|dhānān
karṇe śīdhuṃ tava racayitā
Lakṣmaṇaś cāpa|ghoṣaiḥ.

rakṣo|mauli|stabaka|lavanād
vaira|bandhe vimukte,
gatvā c' ôrvīṃ gagana|padavī|
svairiṇā Puṣpakeṇa,
siddh'|ārambhau sapadi bhavatām
ādhirājy'|âbhiṣekāt
saṃprāpsyāvaś cira|virahataḥ
saṃcitān, devi, bhogān.

2.45 citte kuryāt tad api bhavatī,
yaj Janasthāna|yuddhāt
saṃprāptaṃ māṃ Daśamukha|samān
pārayitvā Khar'|ādīn,
śastr'|āghātaṃ stana|kalaśayor
ūṣmaṇā ropayadbhir
gāḍh'|āśleṣair apihitavatī
gadgadā harṣa|bāṣpaiḥ.

We'll build a massive bridge, using mountain slabs
and arrows that drive back the ocean. We'll turn Lanka
into a playground for the monkeys. In a matter of days,
my brother Lákshmana will engage those monsters
in battle.
The constant twang of his bow will be
music to your ears.

We'll soon be going home. Let me just pluck off
Rávana's mushrooming heads and cut the knot
of enmity. We'll take off in his Púshpaka jet.
We'll make a new beginning. The elders
will waste no time in crowning me king,
and then we'll finally make up for all that we missed
while apart.

You will remember, my queen, the day I returned 2.45
from the battle in Jana·sthana, when I finished off Khara
and a few other demons, who were just like Rávana—
how you healed my wounds with the hot touch
of your breasts and, sobbing for joy,
hugged and hid me
from the world.

Śacyāḥ kleśaṃ kva cana samaye
tādṛśaṃ cintayitvā,
smṛtvā devīm acala|tanayāṃ
viprayuktāṃ Śivena,
rakṣ' ātmānaṃ katham api, śubhe,
jīvit'|ālambanaṃ me.
patyuś chandād vyasanam api hi
ślāghanīyaṃ vadhūnāṃ.› »

apy etat te manasi nihitaṃ
sāhyam a|vyāja|bandhoḥ
pratyākhyātuṃ prabhavati na khalv
ānṛśaṃsyaṃ tvadīyaṃ?
prāg apy evaṃ pariṇata|guṇāṃ
Naiṣadhe vīkṣya vārtāṃ,
ārta|trāṇaṃ vratam iti vidur,
hanta, śuddh'|ātmanāṃ vaḥ.

itthaṃ hṛdyair Janaka|tanayāṃ
jīvayitvā vacobhiḥ,
sakhyaṃ puṣyan dina|kara|kule
dīpyamānair nar'|êndraiḥ,
svairaṃ lokān vicara nikhilān,
saumya, Lakṣmy" êva Viṣṇuḥ
sarv'|ākārais tvad|anuguṇayā
sevito rāja|haṃsyā.

Shachi, Indra's queen, went through it too.
Keep that in mind. And remember, even Párvati
was once severed from Shiva. Take good care
of yourself, you must find a way, my dear,
my life depends on you. Everyone will tell you:
suffering that comes from following your husband
is part of the deal.'"

Final Words to the Goose

You cannot refuse, can you? You're simply too kind.
You'll rise to the task that I planted
in your mind. You're a true friend to me.
Anyone who knows the story of Nala
knows that you geese are committed to lifesaving
    missions
and always see them through.*

Once you've brought Sita back to life
with my well-chosen words, and deepened
your bond with the splendid kings
of the solar line, you can roam freely
through all worlds. You'll be joined,
my dear gander, by your Queen Goose,
perfectly attuned to you in all ways
like Lakshmi to Vishnu.

saṃdiśy' âivaṃ, saha kapi|kulaiḥ
setunā laṅghit'|âbdhiḥ,
Paṅktigrīve yudhi vinihate,
prāpya Sītāṃ pratītaḥ,
rājyaṃ bhūyaḥ svayam anubhavan
rakṣitaṃ pādukābhyāṃ,
Rāmaḥ śrīmān atanuta nijāṃ
rāja|dhānīṃ sa|nāthāṃ.

2.50 vidyā|śilpa|praguṇa|matinā
Veṅkaṭeśena kḷptaṃ,
cintā|śāṇ'|ôllikhitam a|sakṛc,
chreyasāṃ prāpti|hetuṃ,
Sītā|Rāma†|vyatikara|sakhaṃ
Rāma|saṃdeśa|ratnaṃ
paśyantv antaḥ śravaṇam an|aghaṃ
cakṣur ujjīvya santaḥ.

2.50 *rāma* HSalt : *haṃsa* HSed

Epilogue

So much for the message. Rama, never without Fortune,
went on to cross over the sea with his monkey troops
by the bridge they had built. In battle, he lopped off
Rávana's many heads. He reunited with Sita. He was
happy.
He got back the kingdom, where his sandals had reigned
in his absence. From then on, his city never
lacked a king.

This jewel of a poem, The Mission of the Goose, 2.50
was crafted by Venkatésha, whose mind is sharpened
by science and art. It was tested on the touchstone
of deep thought. It confers blessings over and over.
It has the power to bring Rama and Sita together.
Study it closely, you who are wise. Open your eyes
to its beauty, fill your ears with its sounds.

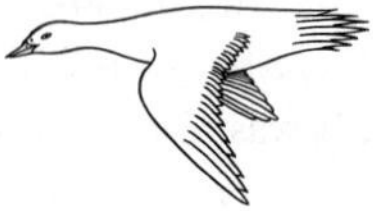

COMPASSION

1 PRAPADYE TAṂ girim prāyaḥ
Śrīnivās'|ânukampayā
ikṣu|sāra|sravanty" êva
yan|mūrtyā śarkarāyitam.

vigāhe tīrtha|bahulām
śītalāṃ guru|saṃtatim
Śrīnivāsa|day"|âmbodhi|
parīvāha|paramparām.

kṛtinaḥ Kamal"|āvāsa|
kāruṇy'|âikāntino bhaje,
dhatte yat|sūkti|rūpeṇa
tri|vedī sarva|yogyatām.

Parāśara|mukhān vande
Bhagīratha|naye sthitān
Kamalākānta|kāruṇya|
Gaṅgā|plāvita|mad|vidhān.

5 a|śeṣa|vighna|śamanaṃ
anīk'|ēśvaram āśraye
Śrīmataḥ karuṇ"|âmbodhau
śikṣā|srota iv' ôtthitam

Prelude

I SURRENDER TO this mountain, 1
this stream of sugar-cane sap
turned solid, as God's Compassion
takes crystal form.

I swim in the cool
steady flood of God's Compassion,
in its deep pools, eddies, currents
flowing through the long line
of our teachers, which
never fails.

I follow unique poets
immersed in the mercy of Kámala's lord.
It is only their songs
that open up all three Vedas
for everyone to hear.

I hold high those sages,
starting with Paráshara,*
who take their lead from the man
who brought the Ganges down to earth.*
The river that is God's Compassion
swept them away
as she now floods me.

I pray to God's General, Vishvak·sena, 5
who washes all obstacles away.
He rises, steady, from the ocean of God's Compassion
like a river flowing uphill.

samasta|jananīṃ vande
caitanya|stanya|dāyinīṃ,
śreyasīṃ Śrīnivāsasya
karuṇām iva rūpiṇīṃ.

vande Vṛṣa|gir'|īśasya
mahiṣīṃ viśva|dhāriṇīṃ,
tat|kṛpā|pratighātānāṃ
kṣamayā vāraṇaṃ yayā.

niśāmayatu māṃ Nīlā
yad|bhoga|paṭalair dhruvaṃ
bhāvitaṃ Śrīnivāsasya
bhakta|doṣeṣv a|darśanaṃ.

kam apy an|avadhiṃ vande
karuṇā|Varuṇ'|ālayaṃ
Vṛṣa|śaila|taṭa|sthānāṃ
svayaṃ vyaktim upāgataṃ.

She mothers all there is.
She nourishes us with the milk
they call awareness.
I bow to her, Compassion embodied,
the best thing about God.

And to Earth, the highest queen
of the Lord of Bull Hill.*
She bears us all
and bears with us all.
She won't let us strike back
at God's Compassion.

Nila,* I pray for your attention.
When God makes love to you,
we can be sure his eyes turn blind
to the faults that we, who love him,
may commit.

That unfathomable, unending
ocean of kindness
who makes himself visible
to anyone who climbs the slopes
of Bull Hill—
I bow to him.

a|kiṃcana|nidhiṃ, sūtim
    apavarga|tri|vargayoḥ
Añjan'|âdr'|īśvara|dayām
    abhiṣṭaumi nir|añjanām.

anucara|śakty|ādi|guṇām,
    agre|sara|bodha|viracit'|ālokāṃ,
sv'|âdhīna|Vṛṣa|gir'|īśāṃ,
    svayaṃ prabhūtāṃ pramāṇayāmi dayāṃ.

api nikhila|loka|su|carita|
    muṣṭiṃ|dhaya|durita|mūrcchan'|â|juṣṭaṃ
saṃjīvayatu, daye, māṃ
    Añjana|giri|nātha|rañjanī bhavatī.

I praise you, Compassion, 10
who belong to the god of Ánjana Hill:*
You are pure gold
to those who own nothing.
You alone deliver final freedom
and the other three ends of men.

Power and other such traits
follow her everywhere.
The light of wisdom
goes before her.
The Lord of Bull Hill
is her servant.
That's how I recognize Compassion
when she comes to be
of her own accord.

I've been bad.
I'm losing my mind.
My terrible record
is a fist in the face
of any good deeds
that others have done.
Mother Compassion! Bring me back
to life. Be the lover
of the god on Ánjana Hill.

bhagavati daye, bhavatyā
Vṛṣa|giri|nāthe samāplute tuṅge
a|pratigha|majjanānāṃ
hast'|ālambo mad|āgasāṃ mṛgyaḥ.

kṛpaṇa|jana|kalpa|latikāṃ
kṛt'|âparādhasya niṣkriyām ādyāṃ,
Vṛṣa|giri|nātha|daye, tvāṃ
vidanti saṃsāra|tāriṇīṃ vibudhāḥ.

Vṛṣa|giri|gṛha|medhi|guṇāḥ
bodha|bal'|āiśvarya|vīrya|śakti|mukhāḥ
doṣā bhaveyur ete
yadi nāma, daye, tvayā vinā|bhūtāḥ.

ā|sṛṣṭi|saṃtatānām
aparādhānāṃ nirodhinīṃ jagataḥ,
Padmāsahāya|karuṇe,
pratisaṃcara|kelim ācarasi.

When you flood even the god
on the peak of Bull Hill,
surely my burden of evil
will drown, too.
Compassion, great goddess:
would it be too much to ask you
to give it a hand?

You're bounty unending
to anyone in want,
immediate expiation
for anyone who's done wrong.
Goddess Compassion who lives with the god
on Bull Hill: those who know,
know you can guide us
to the other shore.

Omniscience, might, mastery, vigor,
and all the other blessed qualities
of the god at home on Bull Hill
would be nothing but a curse, Compassion,
if not for you.

People commit crimes non-stop
from the beginning of time, and you,
God's Compassion, block them with a torrent
at every end of time, as the curtain falls
on your dance.*

a|cid|a|viśiṣṭān pralaye
jantūn avalokya jāta|nirvedā
karaṇa|kalevara|yogaṃ
vitarasi, Vṛṣa|śaila|nātha|karuṇe, tvaṃ.

anuguṇa|daś"|ârpitena,
Śrīdhara|karuṇe, samāhita|*snehā*
śamayasi tamaḥ prajānāṃ
śāstramayena sthira|pradīpena.

rūḍhā Vṛṣ'|âcala|pateḥ
pāde mukha|kānti|patrala|cchāyā,
karuṇe, sukhayasi vinatān
kaṭ'|âkṣa|viṭapaiḥ kar'|âpaceya|phalaiḥ.

nayane Vṛṣ'|âcal'|êndos
tārā|maitrīṃ dadhānayā, karuṇe,
dṛṣṭas tvay" âiva janimān
apavargam a|kṛṣṭa|pacyam anubhavati.

samay'|ôpanatais tava pravāhair,
anukampe, kṛta|saṃplavā dharitrī
śaraṇ'|āgata|sasya|mālin" îyaṃ
Vṛṣa|śail'|ēśa|kṛṣīvalaṃ dhinoti.

Then, after the deluge, when you see all living beings
no better than dead matter, you despair, Compassion,
and bless them with the burden of vital senses
and a body—you
who belong to the god of Bull Hill.

With the unwavering lamp of Scripture,
its coiled wick lit at the right moment
and burning with your love,
you, Mother Compassion, dispel the darkness
in people's minds.

If God is a tree on Bull Hill,
you grow at his feet, you're the lush shade
flowing from the foliage at his head,
and to delight those who bow to him, Compassion,
you bend the long boughs that are his glances
heavy with fruit within reach.

God, rising like the moon on Bull Hill,
supplies the eyes, but you, Compassion,
give him sight. If your gentle gaze falls,
star-like, on anyone alive, they'll find freedom,
a rich yield from an untilled land.

When the earth is flooded on time
by you, Compassion,
pilgrims crop up in field after field
to the great joy of that Peasant
who farms Bull Hill.*

kalaś'|ôdadhi|saṃpado bhavatyāḥ,
karuṇe, san|mati|mantha|saṃskṛtāyāḥ
amṛt'|âṃśam avaimi divya|dehaṃ
mṛta|saṃjīvanam Añjan'|âcal'|êndoḥ.

jala|dher iva śītatā, daye, tvaṃ
Vṛṣa|śail'|âdhipateḥ sva|bhāva|bhūtā.
pralay'|ārabhaṭī|naṭīṃ tad|īkṣāṃ
prasabhaṃ grāhayasi prasatti|lāsyaṃ

praṇata|pratikūla|mūla|ghātī
pratighaḥ ko 'pi Vṛṣ'|âcal'|ēśvarasya
kalame yavas'|âpacāya|nītyā,
karuṇe, kiṃkaratāṃ tav' ôpayāti.

25 a|bahiṣ|kṛta|nigrahān vidantaḥ
Kamalākānta|guṇān sva|tantrat"|ādīn,
a|vikalpam anugrahaṃ duhānāṃ
bhavatīm eva, daye, bhajanti santaḥ.

When you whipped yourself into cream
in the butter-churn of your willing mind,
Compassion, Ocean of Milk,
a spoonful became God's body
rising like the moon on Bull Hill
that pulls the dead
back to life.*

Like coolness to the ocean,
you, Compassion, are the very nature
of the god on Bull Hill.
When his gaze does the wild dance
that devastates the world,
you sternly retrain it
in the soft step of peace.

Someone always has to weed a field
of growing paddy. God's infinite rage
that uproots the enemies
of those who come to him
at Bull Hill takes its orders
from you, Compassion.

Good people know
that among his other fine features,
God is wholly free—but not quite free
from judgment. That's why
they stick to your free-flowing
kindness, Compassion,
no questions asked.

Kamalānilayas tvayā dayāluḥ,
  karuṇe, niṣ|karuṇā nirūpaṇe tvam.
ata eva hi tāvak'|āśritānāṃ
  duritānāṃ bhavati tvad eva bhītiḥ.

atilaṅghita|śāsaneṣv abhīkṣṇaṃ
  Vṛṣa|śail'|âdhipatir vijṛmbhit'|ôṣmā.
punar eva, daye, kṣamā|nidānair
  bhavatīm ādriyate bhavaty|adhīnaiḥ

karuṇe, duriteṣu māmakeṣu
  pratikār'|ântara|dur|jayeṣu khinnaḥ,
kavacāyitayā tvay" âiva Śārṅgī
  vijaya|sthānam upāśrito Vṛṣ'|âdriṃ.

mayi tiṣṭhati duṣ|kṛtāṃ pradhāne,
  mita|doṣān itarān vicinvatī tvam
aparādha|gaṇair a|pūrṇa|kukṣiḥ,
  Kamalākānta|daye kathaṃ bhavitrī?

Since God has you, Compassion,
they call him "the Compassionate."
But come to think of it, you're quite merciless.
Why else would the misdeeds
of those who pray to you
tremble in panic?

Time and again we break the rules
and the God of Bull Hill boils with rage.
But then you marshal the reasons
for having patience, Compassion,
and make him mindful, once more,
of you.

God's depressed. He's tried everything,
but nothing stops me from doing wrong.
That's why he's come here, bow in hand,
to Bull Hill, his last bastion,
where you and only you, Goddess Compassion,
can defend him.

Look at me. I'm the worst of the worst.
If you look to others, with their meager supply of flaws,
how will you survive?
Compassion! Even a hoard of hard-core sins
hardly fills your belly.

aham asmy aparādha|cakravartī,
karuṇe, tvaṃ ca guṇeṣu sārvabhaumī.
viduṣī sthitim īdṛśīṃ svayaṃ māṃ
Vṛṣa|śail'|ēśvara|pādasāt kuru tvaṃ.

a|śithila|karaṇe 'sminn a|kṣata|śvāsa|vṛttau
vapuṣi gamana|yogye vāsam āsādayeyaṃ
Vṛṣa|giri|kaṭakeṣu vyañjayatsu pratītair,
Madhu|mathana|daye, tvāṃ vāri|dhārā|viśeṣaiḥ

a|vidita|nija|yoga|kṣemam, ātm'|ân|abhijñaṃ,
guṇa|lava|rahitaṃ māṃ goptu|kāmā, daye, tvaṃ
paravati caturais te vibhramaiḥ Śrīnivāse
bahu|matim an|apāyāṃ vindasi Śrī|Dharaṇyoḥ.

phala|vitaraṇa|dakṣaṃ,
pakṣa|pāt'|ân|abhijñaṃ,
praguṇam, anuvidheyaṃ
prāpya Padmāsahāyaṃ
mahati guṇa|samāje

I'm the king of wrongdoing,
and you, Compassion, are the Empress
of everything right. You know the balance
of power. Find some way to corner me
at the feet of the god on Bull Hill.

Now,
while my senses are still sharp,
my lungs strong, and my legs can climb,
let me find a home on the slopes of Bull Hill.
I'll see you there, Compassion,
wed to Madhu's Killer,*
in the rush of river and cascade.

I don't know what's good for me.
I know nothing of myself.
There's not an iota of goodness in me,
and still, Compassion, you want to save me.
Lucky that God himself is under the sway
of your arts and wiles, and that both your co-wives,
Fortune above and Earth below,
think the world of you.

He's capable of handing down the verdict.
Utterly impartial.
Highly professional, yet approachable.
In a courtroom packed with principles,
God sits in judgment.
My misdeeds—the prosecution team—

mānalpūrvaṃ, daye, tvaṃ
prativadasi yath"|ârhaṃ
pāpmanāṃ māmakānāṃ.

anubhavitum agh'|âughaṃ n' âlam āgāmi|kālaḥ;
praśamayitum a|śeṣaṃ niṣkriyābhir na śakyaṃ.
svayam iti hi, daye, tvaṃ svī|kṛta|Śrīnivāsā
śithilita|bhava|bhītiḥ śreyase jāyase naḥ.

35 avataraṇa|viśeṣair ātma|līl"|âpadeśair
avamatim, anukampe, manda|citteṣu vindan
Vṛṣabha|śikhari|nāthas tvan|nideśena nūnaṃ
bhajati śaraṇa|bhājāṃ bhāvino janma|bhedān.

para|hitam, anukampe,
bhāvayantyāṃ bhavatyāṃ
sthiram an|upadhi hārdaṃ
Śrīnivāso dadhānaḥ,
lalita|ruciṣu Lakṣmī|
Bhūmi|Nīlāsu nūnaṃ

and all the evidence
are dead against me.
Now you, Compassion,
my able attorney, rising to speak
at the last moment,
will get me off the hook.

The future's not long enough
to wear away my endless crimes.
There's no way I could atone
and put them all to rest. If you weren't there
for me, Compassion, of your own accord,
overruling God, I'd be too afraid
to breathe.

The god on top of Bull Hill
pretends he does it for fun. But really
it's you, Compassion, who mastermind
his odd incarnations
among fools who despise him.
Perhaps you want him to use up
all the lives in store for us
who live at his feet.

Caring for others
is all you care about, Compassion.
That's why God holds you in his heart
with a steady, selfless love.
And if he sometimes shows respect
to the charming trio of his wives—
Fortune, Earth, and the Dark One—

prathayati bahu|mānaṃ
  tvat|praticchanda|buddhyā.

Vṛṣa|giri|savidheṣu vyājato vāsa|bhājāṃ
  durita|kaluṣitānāṃ dūyamānā, daye, tvaṃ
karaṇa|vilaya|kāle kāndiśīka|smṛtīnāṃ
  smarayasi bahu|līlaṃ Mādhavaṃ s'|âvadhānā.

diśi diśi gati|vidbhir deśikair nīyamānā ,
  sthirataram, anukampe, styāna|lagnā guṇais tvaṃ,
parigata|Vṛṣa|śailaṃ pāram āropayantī
  bhava|jaladhi|gatānāṃ pota|pātrī bhavitrī.

parimita|phala|saṃgāt prāṇinaḥ kiṃ|pacānāḥ
  nigama|vipaṇi|madhye nitya|*mukt'*|ânuṣaktaṃ
prasadanam, anukampe, prāptavatyā bhavatyā
  Vṛṣa|giri|hari|nīlaṃ vyañjitaṃ nirviśanti.

it's only because he sees you
in them.

There are those who live near Bull Hill
for all the wrong reasons, their lives blackened
by bad ways. You feel for them too.
When their senses disperse and their fugitive minds
have nowhere to go, and God
is playing his games, you, Compassion,
ever mindful, remind them
of each other.*

At the helm are our teachers,
who know the way. Your qualities
are the thick ropes that hold it together.
The destination: Bull Hill, on the other side
of the sea of life. Be our Boat,
Compassion. Bring us safely
ashore.

Most people are paupers,
scrounging for scraps
in the marketplace of holy texts,
until you open your heart, Compassion,
and spread your wares:
shining pearls, precious souls,*
and the blue sapphire from Bull Hill,
a feast free
for the asking.

tvayi bahu|mati|hīnaḥ Śrīnivās'|ânukampe
jagati gatim ih' ânyāṃ, devi, saṃmanyate yaḥ,
sa khalu Vibudhasindhau saṃnikarṣe vahantyāṃ
śamayati mṛga|tṛṣṇā|vīcikābhiḥ pipāsāṃ.

ājñāṃ, khyātiṃ, dhanam, anucarān,
ādhirājy'|ādikaṃ vā
kāle dṛṣṭvā Kamalavasater
apy a|kiṃcit|karāṇi.
Padmākāntaṃ praṇihitavatīṃ
pālane 'n|anya|sādhye
sār'|âbhijñā jagati kṛtinaḥ
saṃśrayante, daye, tvāṃ.

Prājāpatya|prabhṛti|vibhavaṃ
prekṣya paryāya|duḥkhaṃ,
janm' ākāṅkṣan Vṛṣa|giri|vane
jagmuṣāṃ tasthuṣāṃ vā,
āśāsānāḥ kati cana Vibhos
tvat|pariṣvaṅga|dhanyair
aṅgī|kāraṃ kṣaṇam api, daye,
hārda|tuṅgair apāṅgaiḥ.

Some think lightly of you, God's compassion,
and look for another way.
Imagine a man lapping at a mirage,
dying of thirst, only
a stone-throw from the Ganges.

Power, fame, riches, pomp, whole kingdoms—
a time comes when they're utterly useless
even to the Creator himself.
Those lucky enough to know the secret
can see it coming, so they come
to you, Compassion.
You'll get God to protect them
like no one else.

Those few who come to see that wealth,
even the wealth of the Creator,
is but another name for suffering,
want only to be born among the living or the still
in the forests of Bull Hill.
They hope, Compassion, that God, excited
by your touch, will take them in—
if only for a second—
from the corner of his love-struck eyes.

nābhī|padma|sphuraṇa|subhagā,
navya|nīl'|ôtpal'|ābhā,
krīḍā|śailaṃ kam api, karuṇe,
vṛṇvatī Veṅkaṭ'|ākhyaṃ,
śītā, nityaṃ prasadanavatī,
śraddadhān'|âvagāhyā,
divyā kā cij jayati mahatī
dīrghikā tāvakīnā.

yasmin dṛṣṭe tad|itara|sukhair
gamyate goṣpadatvaṃ,
satyaṃ, jñānaṃ, tribhir avadhibhir
muktam, ānanda|sindhuṃ
tvat|svī|kārāt tam iha kṛtinaḥ
sūri|vṛnd'|ânubhāvyaṃ,
nity'|â|pūrvaṃ nidhim iva, daye,
nirviśanty Añjan'|âdrau.

sāraṃ labdhvā kam api mahataḥ
Śrīnivās'|âmbu|rāśeḥ,
kāle kāle ghana|rasavatī
kālik" êv', ânukampe,
vyakt'|ônmeṣā Mṛgapati|girau,
viśvam āpyāyayantī,
śīl'|ôpajñaṃ kṣarati bhavatī
śītalaṃ sad|guṇ'|âugham.

The lotus growing from his navel lends its sheen
to the center, the dark nympheas radiate
the color of his limbs, and the water is cool, clear,
always inviting for those who dive in
with a ready heart. No words can capture
this pool that is you, Compassion.
Lucky that you chose to well up
on this playground of a mountain
that happens to be God.

He is an ocean of delight.
Once you see him, all other joys
seem like a puddle
in the hoof-print of a cow.
He is truth and awareness,
free from time, space, and matter,
the reality known to his poets.
And since he's all yours, Compassion,
those fortunate enough to find him—
a treasure ever unexpected—
dwell in ecstasy on Ánjana Hill.

Out of the vast ocean that is God
you drink up an essence
for which I have no words
and then time and again
like a dark rain-cloud, Compassion,
you open yourself up over
Lion Hill.* You nurture us all
with a cool rain of rightness,
the fresh taste of wise resolve.

bhīme nityaṃ bhava|jalanidhau
majjatāṃ mānavānām
ālamb'|ârthaṃ Vṛṣa|giri|patis
tvan|nideśāt prayuṅkte
prajñā|sāraṃ prakṛti|mahatā
mūla|bhāgena juṣṭaṃ,
śākhā|bhedaiḥ su|bhagam, an|aghaṃ,
śāśvataṃ śāstra|pāṇiṃ.

vidvat|sevā|kataka|nikaṣair
vīta|paṅk'|āśayānāṃ
Padmā|kāntaḥ praṇayati, daye,
darpaṇaṃ te sva|śāstraṃ,
līlā|dakṣāṃ tvad|an|avasare
lālayan vipralipsāṃ
māyā|śāstrāṇy api, damayituṃ
tvat|prapanna|pratīpān.

daivāt prāpte Vṛṣa|giri|taṭaṃ
dehini, tvan|nidānāt
«svāmin, pāh'!» îty a|vaśa|vacane
vindati svāpam antyaṃ,
devaḥ Śrīmān diśati, karuṇe,
dṛṣṭim icchaṃs tvadīyām,
udghātena śruti|pariṣadām
uttareṇ' âbhimukhyaṃ.

In the always treacherous
ocean of life, people are drowning.
You have ordered the lord of Bull Hill
to extend the helping hand
of revelation, the essential insight,
eternal, flawless, and alluring,
rooted in primal Nature
and unfolding like the Veda
with its many branches.

To those whose minds have been soaped and scoured
by sitting at the feet of those who know,
Padma's lover offers his true Book,
the mirror image of you, Compassion.
But when you look the other way,
he indulges his penchant for deception
by dishing out bogus tomes
to lure the enemies of all
who pray to you.

Sometimes it happens that a person
finds himself on the slopes of Bull Hill
as he falls into final sleep and,
prompted by you, Compassion,
the words "Help me, God!"
slip from his lips. Then God,
never without Fortune (but ever
in need of your attention),
turns to him with "*Om*"—
the "Yes" that begins all the Vedas—
as his answer.*

śreyaḥ|sūtiṃ sakṛd api, daye,
sammatāṃ yaḥ sakhīṃ te
śīt'|ôdārām alabhata janaḥ
Śrīnivāsasya dṛṣṭiṃ,
dev'|ādīnām ayam anṛṇatāṃ
dehavattve 'pi vindan,
bandhān mukto, balibhir an|agaiḥ
pūryate tat|prayuktaiḥ.

divy'|âpāṅgaṃ diśasi, karuṇe,
yeṣu sad|deśik'|ātmā,
kṣipraṃ prāptā Vṛṣa|giri|patiṃ
Kṣatrabandhv|ādayas te.
viśv'|ācāryā Vidhi|Śiva|mukhāḥ
sv'|âdhikār'|ôparuddhāḥ.
manye, mātā jaḍa iva sute,
vatsalā mādṛśe tvaṃ.

ati|kṛpaṇo 'pi jantur adhigamya, daye, bhavatīm
a|śithila|dharma|setu|padavīṃ rucirām a|cirāt,
a|mita|mah"|ōrmi|jālam atilaṅghya bhav'|âmbunidhiṃ,
bhavati Vṛṣ'|âcal'|ēśa|pada|pattana|nitya|dhanī.

And if even once a man captures God's eye—
cool, gracious, the best possible gift,
in short, your closest ally, Compassion—
he is released from his debts to the gods
and all other creditors, freed from his bonds
and, dining on delicacies from heaven,
lives on in his body.

You're the real teacher, Compassion.
When you lecture with the corner of your eye,
your pupils, even a murderer like Kshatra·bandhu,*
find their way to the lord of Bull Hill
that very instant. While all great professors,
Brahma, Shiva, whoever, are occupied
with their own importance,
you favor dropouts like me
as a mother loves her halfwit child
best of all.

Take the case of the most miserable creature
on earth: if he comes to you, Kind Goddess,
he finds a straight, solid bridge, glittering and polished,
to take him quickly across the ocean of living
with its infinite tides, its towering waves,
and suddenly he finds himself a citizen
in the eternal city at God's feet,
the richest person in the world.

abhimukha|bhāva|saṃpad|
abhisaṃbhavināṃ bhavināṃ
kva cid upalakṣitā kva
cid a|bhaṅgura|gūḍha|gatiḥ,
vi|mala|ras'|āvahā, Vṛ-
ṣa|gir'|īśa|daye, bhavatī
sapadi Sarasvat" îva
śamayaty agham a|pratighaṃ.

api, karuṇe, janasya Taruṇenduvibhūṣaṇatām,
api Kamalāsanatvam, api dhāma Vṛṣ'|âdri|pateḥ,
taratamatā|vaśena tanute nanu te vitatiḥ
para|hita|varṣmaṇā paripacelima|kelimatī.

dhṛta|bhuvanā, daye, tri|vidha|gaty|anukūlatarā ,
Vṛṣa|giri|nātha|pāda|parirambhavatī bhavatī
a|vidita|vaibhav" âpi sura|sindhur iv' ātanute
sakṛd|avagāhamānam apa|tāpam a|pāpam api.

For those lucky beings who come into being
with their hearts turned toward you,
you, Compassion, at times visible,
at others hidden yet steady,
like the river Sarásvati that flows out of sight,
swell, limpid with feeling, to sweep away
the most stubborn stains.

A man can even become Shiva,
crescent moon and all,
or turn into Brahma, seated on his lotus throne,
you can even give him the full power
of the god on Bull Hill.
To each one you're different, Compassion.
To each his own. Aren't these your favorite
escapades? Doing good for others
is what you're all about.

Holding the world together
like the surging River of the Gods,
and spilling out the three great boons*
on the shores of the triple world,
you, Compassion, of depth
unfathomable, hugging God's feet on Bull Hill,
heal the burns and burdens
of anyone who takes
the first plunge.

nigama|samāśritā, ni-
khila|loka|samṛddhi|karī ,
bhajad|agha|kūlam|udru-
ja|gatiḥ, paritapta|hitā,
prakaṭita|haṃsa|matsya|
kamaṭh'|ādy|avatāra|śatā,
Vibudhasaric|chriyaṃ, Vṛ-
ṣa|gir'|īśa|daye, vahasi.

jagati mitaṃ|pacā tvad|
itarā tu, daye, taralā
phala|niyam'|ôjjhitā bha-
vati saṃtapanāya; punaḥ
tvam iha nir|aṅkuśa|pra-
śakan'|ādi|vibhūtimatī
vitarasi dehināṃ nir|
avadhiṃ Vṛṣa|śaila|nidhiṃ.

sa|karuṇa|laukika|prabhu|parigraha|nigrahayor
niyatim upādhi|cakra|parivṛtti|paraṃparayā,
Vṛṣabha|mahīdhar'|ēśa|karuṇe, vitaraṃgayatāṃ
śruti|mita|saṃpadi tvayi kathaṃ bhavitā viśayaḥ?

The old books are unanimous: 55
you're every bit as beautiful
as the Ganges, Compassion
at home on Bull Hill, and like her
you make the whole world
come alive. You smash the levees
and wash away the muddy deeds
of those who love you. And as for the hundred
incarnations, goose, fish, and turtle,
and all the others, they all spring
from you.

In this world there are others
who claim your title, Compassion.
They're all stingy, unreliable,
and of no use. They're more trouble
than they're worth. But you,
with unstinting powers, lavish
on everyone alive
the endless treasure that is
the lord on Bull Hill.

Worldly kings, even the compassionate variety,
are dependably unstable, like a wheel
that never stops turning. They have all kinds
of whims and reasons to punish or to cherish.
Those who have fathomed this will stay afloat,
Compassion alive in the God on Bull Hill,
bounteous by definition: how could they ever
doubt *you*?

Vṛṣa|giri|kṛṣṇa|megha|janitāṃ jani|tāpa|harāṃ
tvad|abhimatiṃ su|vṛṣṭim upajīvya nivṛtta|tṛṣaḥ,
bahuṣu jal'|āśayeṣu bahu|mānam apohya, daye,
na jahati sat|pathaṃ jagati cātakavat kṛtinaḥ.

tvad|udaya|tūlikābhir
amunā Vṛṣa|śaila|juṣā
sthira|cara|śilpin" âiva
parikalpita|citra|dhiyaḥ
Yatipati|Yāmuna|pra-
bhṛtayaḥ prathayanti, daye,
«jagati hitaṃ na nas tva-
yi bhara|nyasanād adhikaṃ.»

60 mṛdu|hṛdaye daye, mṛ-
dita|kāma|hite, mahite,
dhṛta|vibudhe, budheṣu
vitat'|ātma|dhure, madhure,
Vṛṣa|giri|sārvabhauma|
dayite, mayi te mahatīṃ,
bhavuka|nidhe, nidhehi
bhava|mūla|harāṃ laharīṃ.

The Black Cloud on Bull Hill
gives birth to the sweet rain
that is your kindness, that soothes the burns
of being alive. Lucky are those
who quench their thirst with this liquid
compassion, never losing focus,
untempted by the fools' foul water
that fills the world, like the sparrow that lives only
on raindrops.

The great artist resident on Bull Hill
who paints the living and the still
with a set of brushes dipped
in you, Compassion,
has created such brilliant minds as
Ramánuja and Yámuna (to name but two).
They all sing in one voice:
"Nothing in this world feels better
than dumping our burdens
on you."

Tenderness is your second name,
your fame, your game
is caring for anyone
rid of desire. You allow the gods
to be gods and you share
your heart of wisdom
with the wise. You're the sweetheart
of the Emperor on Bull Hill,
Sweet Goddess, a flood
of fortune: so please flood me

akūpārair ek'|ô-
daka|samaya|vaitaṇḍika|javair
a|nirvāpyāṃ kṣipraṃ
kṣapayitum a|vidy"|ākhya|vaḍavāṃ,
kṛpe, tvaṃ tat|tādṛk|
prathima|Vṛṣa|pṛthvīdhara|pati|
sva|rūpa|dvaiguṇya|
dvi|guṇa|nija|binduḥ prabhavasi.

vivitsā|vetālī|
vigama|pariśuddhe 'pi hṛdaye,
paṭu|pratyāhāra|
prabhṛti|puṭa|pāka|pracakitāḥ
namantas tvāṃ, Nārā-
yaṇa|śikhari|kūṭa|stha|karuṇe,
niruddha|tvad|drohā
nṛ|pati|suta|nītiṃ na jahati.

with a wave wild enough to wash away
rebirth.

A whole ocean of reason, vast
as the doomsday flood, can't put out
the fire of ignorance,
burning under the waves.*
But take the entire essence
of the God on Bull Hill
in all his immensity,
double it,
then double it again,
and you'll get
a single drop of Compassion.
That will do.

Even those who have exorcised from their hearts
the vampire called Wanting To Know More
are unnerved by the painfully slow cooking—
reining in the senses and so on and so forth—
that Yoga prescribes. So they simply surrender
to you, Compassion, on the pinnacle
of God's mountain, promising
never to betray you again—
like the prodigal prince from the proverb,
welcomed home by the king.

an|any'|âdhīnaḥ san
bhavati para|tantraḥ praṇamatāṃ;
kṛpe, sarva|draṣṭā
na gaṇayati teṣām apakṛtiṃ;
patis tvat|pārārthyaṃ
prathayati Vṛṣa|kṣmādhara|patir.
vyavasthāṃ vaiyātyād
iti vighaṭayantī viharasi.

apāṃ patyuḥ śatrūn,
a|sahana|muner dharma|nigalaṃ,
kṛpe, kākasy' «âikaṃ
hitam» iti hinasti sma nayanaṃ.
vilīna|svātantryo
Vṛṣa|giri|patis tvad|vihṛtibhir
diśaty evaṃ devo
janita|su|gatiṃ daṇḍana|gatim.†

---

64 *gatim* DSed : *vidhim* DSalt

Though controlled by none,
he's wholly in the power
of those who bow to him.
Seeing everything, as he does,
he is totally blind to their faults.
He's the lord of Bull Hill, and your lord,
too, Compassion, totally under your thumb.
It's all a game for you and, shameless,
you keep on breaking
the rules.

The arrow aimed at the ocean
shot down the enemies of the ocean.
The blow that struck the irascible sage
freed him from the fetters of priggishness.
A dart plucked out the crow's eye—
he's much better off with just one.
When it comes to the lord
of Bull Hill, who's totally free
to play the role you've given him,
Compassion, punishment always
turns to profit.*

65 Niṣādānāṃ netā,
kapi|kula|patiḥ, k" âpi Śabarī,
Kucelaḥ, kubjā sā,
Vraja|yuvatayo, mālya|kṛd iti:
amīṣāṃ nimnatvaṃ
Vṛṣa|giri|pater unnatim api
prabhūtaiḥ srotobhiḥ
prasabham, anukampe, samayasi.

tvayā dṛṣṭas tuṣṭiṃ
bhajati Parameṣṭhī nija|pade;
vahan mūrtīr aṣṭau
viharati Mṛḍānī|paribṛḍhaḥ;
bibharti svārājyaṃ,
Vṛṣa|śikhari|śṛṅgāri|karuṇe,
Śunāsīro dev'|â-
sura|samara|nāsīra|su|bhaṭaḥ.

daye, dugdh'|ôdanvad|
vyatiyuta|sudhā|sindhu|nayatas
tvad|āśleṣān nityaṃ
janita|mṛta|saṃjīvana|daśāḥ,
sva|dante dāntebhyaḥ
śruti|vadana|karpūra|gulikāḥ,
viṣuṇvantaś cittaṃ
Vṛṣa|śikhari|viśvaṃbhara|guṇāḥ.

A hunter chief, a monkey king, 65
one tribal woman, Kuchéla the pauper,
a certain hunchback, the cowgirls of Braj,
one maker of garlands:
what a lowly bunch they are,
and how lofty is the god of Bull Hill,
and yet they all even out
in the fierce floods
of Compassion.*

Once graced by your gaze, Compassion,
lover of the god on Bull Hill,
Brahma is content with his job
as the creator of the world; Shiva,
Párvati's husband, happily turns himself
into the world, from the atoms up;
and Indra, assuming the kingship of heaven,
rushes to do battle with demons
like the lowliest private in the line.

Such are the ways of the god
on Bull Hill, who holds everything together:
when you fill him, like a sea of ecstasy
flowing into an ocean of milk,
he becomes a healing herb
that brings the dead back to life,
a pill of sweet-smelling camphor
on the tongue of those who dare to taste it
straight from the mouth of the Veda,
a constant cure
melting the mind.

jagaj|janma|sthema|
pralaya|racanā|keli|rasiko,
vimukty|eka|dvāraṃ,
vighaṭita|kavāṭaṃ praṇayināṃ—
iti tvayy āyattaṃ
dvitayam upadhī|kṛtya, karuṇe,
viśuddhānāṃ vācāṃ
Vṛṣa|śikhari|nāthaḥ stuti|padaṃ.

Kali|kṣobh'|ônmīlat|
kṣiti|kaluṣa|kūlaṃkaṣa|javair,
an|ucchedair etair
avaṭa|taṭa|vaiṣamya|rahitaiḥ
pravāhais te, Padmā|
sahacara|pariṣkāriṇi kṛpe,
vikalpante† 'n|alpā
Vṛṣa|śikhariṇo nirjhara|gaṇāḥ.†

«khilaṃ ceto|vṛtteḥ
kim idam?» iti vismera|bhuvanaṃ,
kṛpe, Siṃha|kṣmābhṛt|
kṛta|mukha|camatkāra|karaṇaṃ
bhara|nyāsa|cchanna|
prabala|vṛjina|prābhṛta|bhṛtāṃ
pratiprasthānaṃ te
Śruti|nagara|śṛṅgāṭaka|juṣaḥ.

---

69 *vikalpante* DSalt : *vikalpyante* DSed 69 *gaṇāḥ* DSed : *guṇāḥ* DSalt

They say that he is the expert
when it comes to making the world,
or keeping it going, or dissolving it
for fun. They also say that he's the only
door to freedom, and the lock
is broken. Both these accolades rest entirely
on you, Compassion.
You make the lord of Bull Hill worthy
of such fine words.

A torrent that tears down the banks
and carries off the mass of mud
that comes with living in our time,
a flash flood that never stops,
that levels difference
so that high equals low:
Compassion, jewel of Padma's lover,
I see you in the waterfalls
that drench the slopes
of Bull Hill.

What a crazy idea! What's going on?
The whole world smiles in disbelief
and the God on Lion Hill gasps
in admiration when you, Compassion,
stand waiting at the crossroads
of Veda City, to welcome
anyone who turns up in the tattered cloak
of surrender, with nothing to offer
but misdeeds.

tri|vidha|cid|a|cit|
sattā|sthema|pravṛtti|niyāmikā
Vṛṣa|giri|vibhor
icchā sā tvaṃ parair a|parāhatā
kṛpaṇa|bhara|bhṛt|
kiṃ|kurvāṇa|prabhūta|guṇ'|ântarā
vahasi, karuṇe,
vaicakṣaṇyaṃ mad|īkṣaṇa|sāhase.

Vṛṣa|giri|pater
hṛdyā, viśv'|âvatāra|sahāyinī,
kṣapita|nikhil'|â-
vadyā, devi, kṣam"|ādi|niṣevitā,
bhuvana|jananī,
puṃsāṃ bhog'|âpavarga|vidhāyinī,
vi|tamasi pade
vyaktiṃ nityāṃ bibharṣi, daye, svayaṃ.

svayam|udayinaḥ,
siddh'|ādy|āviṣkṛtāś ca śubh'|ālayāḥ,
vividha|vibhava|
vyūh'|āvāsāḥ, paraṃ ca padaṃ vibhoḥ—
Vṛṣa|giri|mukheṣv
eteṣv icch"|âvadhi|pratilabdhaye
dṛḍha|vinihitā
niśreṇis tvaṃ, daye, nija|parvabhiḥ.

Conscious and unconscious beings
come in threes,* and each has three phases:
self, being, action. You, Compassion,
control them all. You're the active will
of the lord on Bull Hill, and no one
can stop you. All his other parts
are your lowly porters and slaves,
and still, driven by the wildest
of whims, your eyes are fixed
on me.

Closest to the heart of the lord of Bull Hill,
you keep him company whenever he comes
down to earth. You erase despicable deeds.
Patience and her friends wait upon you.
Mother of the world, you parcel out both
joys of the body and final freedom
to your creatures. You're a palpable presence
on every luminous stage.

God lives in many shapes and homes:
some pop up by themselves, some are uncovered
by seers and their like, some host
the oldest emanations* and other famous forms,
and then there's the highest place of all—
and in all of them, starting with Bull Hill,
you are firmly in place, Compassion,
a ladder of endless rungs,
so we can climb as high
as we like.

hitam iti jagad|
drṣṭyā kḷptair, a|kḷpta|phal'|ântarair,
a|mati|vihitair
anyair, dharmāyitaiś ca yadṛcchayā,
pariṇata|bahu|
cchadmā, Padmā|sahāya|daye, svayaṃ
pradiśasi nij'|â-
bhipretaṃ naḥ praśāmyad|apatrapā.

ati|vidhi|śivair
aiśvary'|ātm'|ânubhūti|rasair janān
a|hṛdayam ih' ô-
pacchandy' âiṣām a|saṃga|daś"|ârthinī
tṛṣita|janatā|
tīrtha|snāna|krama|kṣapit'|âinasāṃ
vitarasi, daye,
vīt'|ātaṅkā Vṛṣ'|âdri|pateḥ padaṃ.

Vṛṣa|giri|sudhā|
sindhau jantur, daye, nihitas tvayā
bhava|bhaya|parī-
tāpa|cchittyai bhajann agha|marṣaṇaṃ
muṣita|kaluṣo
mukter agre|sarair abhipūryate
svayam upanataiḥ
sv'|ātm'|ānanda|prabhṛty|anubandhibhiḥ.

We do all sorts of things: some, we think,
must be of use, though we have no clue
as to their true effects. Some we do
without thinking. Some, by chance, are even
somewhat decent. And you, Compassion,
beloved of Padma's lover, have the nerve
to give us whatever we ask for
and to claim that we've earned it
by doing this or that.

Greater than Brahma and Shiva combined 75
are the potions of mastery and self-possession*
that you entice us to taste. So occupied
are you with our freedom that you, Compassion,
couldn't care less, you have no qualms
about giving us the keys
to god's home on Bull Hill.
Sometimes a man thirsts only for a sip
of water and ends up bathing
in a river that washes away
all stains.

You take a creature and put him up
on Bull Hill, that ocean of sweetness
where he cuts the fearful knot of birth
and washes off the dirt of his deeds.
Open and clean, he can feast on
the pleasures that herald final freedom
and those that come with it—
self-rapture, for a start.

an|itara|juṣām
    antar|mūle 'py apāya|pariplave
  kṛta|vid an|aghā
    vicchidy' âiṣāṃ, kṛpe, Yama|vaśyatāṃ,
prapadana|phala|
    pratyādeśa|prasaṅga|vivarjitaṃ
  prativividhim upā-
    dhatse sārdhaṃ Vṛṣ'|âdri|hit'|âiṣiṇā.

kṣaṇa|vilayināṃ
    śāstr'|ârthānāṃ phalāya niveśite,
  sura|pitṛ|gaṇe
    nirveśāt prāg api pralayaṃ gate,
adhigata|Vṛṣa|
    kṣmābhṛn|nāthām a|kāla|vaśaṃvadāṃ
  pratibhuvam iha
    vyācakhyus tvāṃ, kṛpe, nir|upaplavāṃ.

tvad|upasadanād
    adya śvo vā mahā|pralaye 'pi vā,
  vitarati nijaṃ
    pād'|âmbhojaṃ Vṛṣ'|âcala|śekharaḥ.
tad iha, karuṇe,
    tat|tat|krīḍā|taraṅga|paraṃparā|
  taratamatayā
    juṣṭāyās te dur|atyayatāṃ viduḥ.

Even if someone committed to you
brings trouble upon himself, you,
lucid Compassion,
ever mindful of his one good act,
rescue him from Death's domain.
Together with the kindhearted god
on Bull Hill, you activate the antidote
that ensures, beyond doubt, the full ripening
of surrender.

All the promises of the scriptures have a date
of expiration. The gods and the ancestors
are in charge of handing out rewards,
but before they can even begin, they too
expire. As for you, Compassion,
defying time, immune to circumstance,
the lord of Bull Hill under your wing:
poets sing of you as the one
sure thing.

We come to you—so today, or tomorrow,
or at worst, at the end of time, God
on the summit of Bull Hill will take us
to his feet, soft as flowers. In the meantime,
Compassion, everyone knows how you like
to play with this and that, wave
after wave, riptide and tide,
though no one touches
your depth.

80 praṇihita|dhiyāṃ
tvat|saṃpṛkte Vṛṣ'|âdri|śikhā|maṇau,
prasṛmara|sudhā|
dhār"|ākārā prasīdati bhāvanā.
dṛḍham iti, daye,
datt'|āsvādaṃ vimukti|valāhakaṃ
nibhṛta|garuto
nidhyāyanti sthir'|āśaya|cātakāḥ.

kṛpe, vigata|velayā kṛta|samagra|poṣais tvayā
Kali|jvalana|dur|gate jagati kāla|meghāyitaṃ
Vṛṣa|kṣitidhar'|ādiṣu sthiti|padeṣu s'|ânuplavair
Vṛṣ'|âdri|pati|vigrahair vyapagat'|â|khil'|âvagrahaiḥ.

prasūya vividhaṃ jagat, tad|abhivṛddhaye tvaṃ, daye,
samīkṣaṇa|vicintana|prabhṛtibhiḥ svayaṃ tādṛśaiḥ
vicitra|guṇa|citritāṃ, vividha|doṣa|vaideśikīṃ
Vṛṣ'|âcala|pates tanuṃ viśasi matsya|kūrm'|ādikāṃ.

When we fix our mind on that Jewel
of Bull Hill, set in you, Compassion,
a certain vision becomes clear, limpid
as a steady stream. We're like the birds
who live on raindrops, not moving
a feather, our whole being turned toward
the cloud that surely tastes
of release.

The world is ablaze with the fire
of our times. You, Compassion
without limit, take all the living forms
of God on Bull Hill from there
and other worthy places, servants
and all, endow them with everything
they need, and turn them into one big
black cloud that will never
dry up.

First you gave birth to the entire world.
Then, to keep it going, you, Compassion,
enter the body of the god on Bull Hill
in whatever avatar, be it a fish,
be it a tortoise. You take this marvel
of many modes, impervious
to imperfection, and make it
see and think
and all the rest.

yug'|ânta|samay'|ôcitaṃ bhajati yoga|nidrā|rasaṃ
Vṛṣa|kṣitibhṛd|īśvare, viharaṇa|kramāj jāgrati,
udīrṇa|catur|arṇavī|kadana|vedinīṃ medinīṃ
samuddhṛtavatī, daye, tvad|abhijuṣṭayā daṃṣṭrayā.

saṭā|paṭala|bhīṣaṇe,
sa|rabhas'|âṭṭa|hās'|ôdbhaṭe,
sphurat|krudhi, parisphuṭad|
bhru|kuṭike 'pi vaktre kṛte,
daye, Vṛṣa|gir'|īśitur
Danu|ja|ḍimbha|datta|stanā
saroja|sadṛśā dṛśā
samudit'|ākṛtir dṛśyase.

prasakta|madhunā Vidhi|praṇihitaiḥ sapary"|ôdakaiḥ,
samasta|durita|cchidā, nigama|gandhinā tvaṃ, daye,
a|śeṣam a|viśeṣatas tri|jagad Añjan'|âdr'|īśituś
car'|â|caram acīkaraś caraṇa|paṅkajen' âṅkitam.

When the lord on Bull Hill sinks
into sweet sleep at the end of the cycle
of time, waking only when he wants
to play, and Earth screams for help
as all four oceans surge up to drown her,
you, Compassion, raise her
from the depths on the tusk
of the Wild Boar—one tool
of your trade.*

Even when the god on Bull Hill
puts on his most frightening face,
a ferocious scowl, bursting with fury,
a chilling roar of glee, his wild mane
standing on end, even then, Compassion,
you can be seen in his eye,
soft as a lotus petal, nursing
the demon's orphaned child
at your breast.*

Like a lotus flowing with honey 85
is the foot of the god on Ánjana Mountain.
Brahma waters it each day and, redolent
of the Veda, it undoes all
our misdeeds. As for you,
Compassion, you've taken that foot
and imprinted it high and low, all through
this triple world, making no distinction
between the sentient and the still.*

paraśvatha*|tapodhana|prathana|sat|krat'|ûpākṛta|
kṣit'|īśvara|paśu|kṣarat|kṣata|ja|kuṅkuma|sthāsakaiḥ
Vṛṣ'|âcala|dayālunā nanu vihartum ālipyathāḥ
nidhāya hṛdaye, daye, nihata|rakṣitānāṃ hitam.

kṛpe, kṛta|jagadd|hite, kṛpaṇa|jantu|cintā|maṇe!
Ramā|sahacaraṃ kṣitau Raghu|dhurīṇayantyā tvayā
vyabhajyata sarit|patiḥ sakṛd|avekṣaṇāt tat|kṣaṇāt
prakṛṣṭa|bahu|pātaka|praśama|hetunā setunā.

kṛpe, paravatas tvayā Vṛṣa|gir'|īśituḥ krīḍitaṃ
jagadd|hitam a|śeṣatas. tad idam ittham arthāpyate
mada|cchala|paricyuta|praṇata|duṣ|kṛta|prekṣitair
hata|prabala|dānavair Haladharasya helā|śataiḥ.

When the Sage with the Axe held the great
sacrifice of war, and all the kings of the earth
were offered up as victims, you,
Compassion, were splattered
with the saffron paste of their blood
by that kind soul on Bull Hill, playing
his usual tricks. Still you held close
to your heart all those who were slain
and thus saved.*

Compassion! You're the wellbeing
of this world, a philosopher's stone
in the hands of every poor creature.
You're the one who made Lakshmi's
Lover take up the burden
of being Rama on earth and split
the sea in two with the vast bridge
that puts all evil to rest as soon
as we see it, once and for all.*

Compassion! Because of you, the god
on Bull Hill, utterly in your power,
plays his games for the good of the world
and nothing else. If you need proof,
consider the hundred wiles of Bala·rama,*
who bears the plow. He's sober enough
to kill the mightiest of demons but drunk
enough not to see the dark side
of those who love him.

prabhūta|vibudha|dviṣad|
bharaṇa|khinna|viśvaṃbharā|
bhar'|âpanayana|cchalāt
tvam avatārya Lakṣmī|dharaṃ,
nirākṛtavatī, daye,
nigama|saudha|dīpa|śriyā
vipaścid|a|vigītayā
jagati Gītay" ândhaṃ tamaḥ.

90 Vṛṣ'|âdri|haya|sādinaḥ prabala|dor|marut|preṅkhitas,
tviṣā|sphuṭa|taḍid|guṇas, tvad|avaseka|saṃskāravān
kariṣyati, daye, Kali|prabala|gharma|nirmūlanaḥ
punaḥ Kṛta|yug'|âṅkuraṃ bhuvi kṛpāṇa|dhārā|dharaḥ.

viśv'|ôpakāram iti nāma sadā duhānām
ady' âpi, devi, bhavatīm avadhīrayantaṃ
nāthe niveśaya, Vṛṣ'|âdri|pater daye, tvaṃ
nyasta|sva|rakṣaṇa|bharaṃ tvayi māṃ tvay" âiva.

After all this, you brought Lakshmi's Husband
down to our world yet again. The excuse
this time was that too many of God's enemies
were prowling around, and poor Earth,
who bears everything, could bear
no more. Some simply had to be removed.
But really, Compassion, it was to dispel
all darkness by making him sing
that Song,* the most brilliant lamp
in the vast palace of the Vedas,
the one the learned adore.

When the lord on Bull Hill mounts
his Doomsday horse, the sword he swings
in his powerful arm—a rain-cloud
driven by the wind, flashing
with a lightning sheen and washed
clean by your blessings—will banish
the burning heat of this dark age
and let a golden new time
sprout again.*

If it's good for the world, it comes from you.
I'm the one who ignores you
even now. Please, Compassion, open
the doors to God on Bull Hill
and let me in. The burden
of caring for me rests solely
in your hands. And who put it there?
No one but you.

naisargikeṇa tarasā, karuṇe, niyuktā
  nimn'|êtare 'pi mayi te vitatir yadi syāt,
vismāpayed Vṛṣa|gir'|īśvaram apy, a|vāryā
  vel"|âtilaṅghana|daś" êva mah"|âmbu|rāśeḥ.

vijñāta|śāsana|gatir viparīta|vṛttyā
  Vṛtr'|ādibhiḥ paricitāṃ padavīṃ bhajāmi.
evaṃ|vidhe, Vṛṣa|gir'|īṣa|daye, mayi tvaṃ
  dīne vibhoḥ śamaya daṇḍa|dharatva|līlāṃ.

mā|sāhas'|ôkti|ghana|kañcuka|vañcit'|ânyaḥ
  paśyatsu teṣu vidadhāmy ati|sāhasāni.
Padmā|sahāya|karuṇe, na ruṇatsi kiṃ tvaṃ
  ghoraṃ kuliṅga|śakuner iva ceṣṭitaṃ me?

95 vikṣepam arhasi, daye, vipalāyite 'pi,
  vyājaṃ vibhāvya Vṛṣa|śaila|pater vihāraṃ.

I'm quite a lofty fellow, but if, Compassion,
with your instinctive force, you rise up
to submerge me, God himself won't believe
his eyes—like when an ocean surges far
beyond the shore with nothing
to stop it.

I know what the books say about
how to live. I do just the opposite.
I follow the well-trod path of Vritra
and other famous monsters.
These are the facts, Compassion.
I'm pathetic. It's up to you to hold back
the lord on Bull Hill, who's just itching
to let me have it.

"Don't risk your neck!"—That's my line,
the alibi I wear on my sleeve.
Then recklessly I risk my neck,
time and again, as everyone
can see. Why, for God's sake,
don't you stop me, Compassion?
I'm the sparrow that cries
"Watch out! Watch out!"
while picking scraps
from the lion's teeth.

I run away from you, Compassion.
You've got to trap me, right here
on Bull Hill. Take the Mountain King's
favorite game as your excuse. With the fibers

sv'|âdhīna|sattva|saraṇiḥ svayam atra jantau
drāghīyasī dṛḍhatarā guṇa|vāgurā tvam.

saṃtanyamānam aparādha|gaṇam vicintya
trasyāmi, hanta, bhavatīṃ ca vibhāvayāmi.
ahnāya me, Vṛṣa|gir'|īśa|daye, jah' îmām
āśīviṣa|grahaṇa|keli|nibhām avasthāṃ.

autsukya|pūrvam upahṛtya mah"|âparādhān,
mātaḥ, prasādayitum icchati me manas tvāṃ.
ālihya tān nir|avaśeṣam, a|labdha|tṛptis
tāmyasy, aho Vṛṣa|gir'|īśa|dhṛtā daye, tvaṃ.

jahyād Vṛṣ'|âcala|patiḥ pratighe 'pi na tvāṃ,
gharm'|ôpatapta iva śītalatām udanvān.
sā mām aruntuda|bhara|nyasan'|ânuvṛttis
tad|vīkṣaṇaiḥ spṛśa, daye, tava keli|padmaiḥ.

of his being, weave yourself into a net—
immensely strong and endlessly wide,
wide enough for every living being—
and throw yourself around
this wild animal.*

I say to myself, "The list of my mistakes
seems to go on forever." I get scared.
I invoke you in my mind.
I pray to you, Compassion:
Kill this habit of mine of toying
with poisonous snakes.
Do it today!

First there is longing. Then, Mother,
my heart wants only to please you,
and I offer everything I have—all
my major crimes. You lick them clean,
Compassion, held close by the god
on Bull Hill, and still you're far
from satisfied, hungry
for more.

Even in rage, the lord of Bull Hill
will never desert you, Compassion,
just as the ocean, baked
in the summer sun, never stops
being cool. I know it hurts you
that I keep coming, time and again,
to unload my troubles on you.
Still, I ask you to touch me

dṛṣṭe 'pi dur|bala|dhiyaṃ, damane 'pi dṛptaṃ,
snātv" âpi dhūli|rasikaṃ, bhajane 'pi bhīmaṃ,
baddhvā gṛhāṇa, Vṛṣa|śaila|pater daye, māṃ
tvad|vāraṇaṃ svayam anugraha|śṛṅkhalābhiḥ.

100 n' âtaḥ paraṃ kim api me tvayi nāthanīyaṃ.
mātar, daye, mayi kuruṣva tathā prasādaṃ,
baddh'|ādaro Vṛśagiri|praṇayī yath" âsau
mukt'|ânubhūtim iha dāsyati me Mukundaḥ.

niḥ|sīma|vaibhava|juṣāṃ miṣatāṃ guṇānāṃ
stotur, daye, Vṛṣa|gir'|īśa|gun'|ēśvarīṃ tvāṃ,
tair eva nūnam a|vaśair abhinanditaṃ me.
satyāpitaṃ tava balād a|kuto|bhayatvaṃ.

with his eyes, two lotuses blossoming
in your hand.

What can you do with an elephant
in heat? If you show it the way,
it stubbornly ignores it. It's too proud
to be tamed. Try to bathe it, and it'll dry itself
with dust. Even if you spoil it, it runs
amok. The only way, Compassion,
is to take me and bind me
with the iron shackles
of your mercy.

This is the last thing I'm asking
from you. Mother! Compassion!
Please say yes. Make Mukunda,
that god who fell in love with Bull Hill,
notice me. Make him show me
what's it's like to be free.

Epilogue

Eyes wide open, all the infinite
powers of God on Bull Hill
listened as I sang to you,
most powerful of them all.
Now they're clapping their hands for me—
they can't help it. It turns out, Compassion,
I was right not to be afraid,
pinning my hopes
on you.*

ady' âpi tad, Vṛṣa|gir'|īśa|daye, bhavatyām
   ārambha|mātram an|idaṃ prathama|stutīnām.
saṃdarśita|sva|para|nirvahaṇā sahethāḥ
   mandasya sāhasam idaṃ tvayi vandino me.

prāyo, daye, tvad|anubhāva|mah"|âmbu|rāśau
   Prācetasa|prabhṛtayo 'pi paraṃ taṭa|sthāḥ.
tatr' âvatīrṇam a|tala|spṛśam āplutaṃ māṃ
   Padmā|pateḥ prahasan'|ôcitam ādriyethāḥ.

Vedāntadeśika|pade viniveśya bālaṃ
   devo dayā|śatakam etad avādayan māṃ,
vaihārikeṇa vidhinā samaye gṛhītaṃ
   vīṇā|viśeṣam iva Veṅkaṭa|śaila|nāthaḥ.

Even now, the beginningless hymns
of the Veda have hardly made a beginning
when it comes to praising you, Compassion,
goddess of conclusions: please bear with me
as you bear with others. Forgive this fool
of a poet for his reckless ravings
about you.

Take all those classical poets—from Valmíki on.
They came all the way up
to a vast ocean of experience,
the experience that is you,
but they never even dipped their toes.
Compassion: shouldn't you pay me
some attention? I jumped in,
I can't touch bottom,
I'm drowning, and God
sits there smiling.

The god on Vénkatam Hill took me, a mere child
and gave me a fine title: "Vedánta Déshika,"
Teacher of Final Truth.
Then he spoke through me
these Hundred Verses on Compassion,
as if he'd taken up some lute
that was lying around and,
just for fun, produced
a few notes.

105 an|avadhim adhikṛtya Śrīnivās'|ânukampām,
a|vitatha|viṣayatvād viśvam a|vrīḍayantī,
vividha|kuśala|nīvī, Veṅkaṭeśa|prasūtā
stutir iyam an|avadyā śobhate sattva|bhājām.

śatakam idam udāraṃ samyag abhyasyamānān
Vṛṣa|girim adhiruhya vyaktam ālokayantī,
an|itara|śaraṇānām ādhirājye 'bhiṣiñcet
śamita|vimata|pakṣā Śārṅgadhanv'|ânukampā.

viśv'|ânugraha|mātaraṃ, vyatiṣajat|
svarg'|âpavargāṃ, sudhā|
sadhrīcīm iti Veṅkaṭeśvara|kavir
bhaktyā dayām astuta.
padyānām iha yad|vidheya|bhagavat|
saṃkalpa|kalpa|drumāj
jhaṃjhā|māruta|dhūta|cūta|nayataḥ
sāṃpātiko 'yaṃ kramaḥ.

My faultless poem of praise is all about 105
God's infinite compassion, a topic
that cannot be false. What it reveals
should embarrass no one. It stakes itself
on all the good things in this world.
God Venkatésha gave birth to it.
They will treasure it
who love truth.

When Compassion who belongs to God
with the bow in his hand sees those who
climb Bull Hill, reciting by heart
this noble poem of mine, she'll see them
for who they are. She'll crown them kings
over those who have no other place to go,
who take refuge in her, and put rivalry
to rest.

My name is Venkatéshvara. I'm the poet
who humbly praised Compassion
as the one kind mother of all
there is, who offers you the options
of heaven or final freedom, the pure honey
of life. Don't think I put these poems
in any special order. They came
tumbling out in a single fierce moment.
A hurricane smashed against the wishing tree
that is called "God's intention," that is nothing
but Compassion, and all the mangos
came crashing down.

kāmaṃ santu mithaḥ karambita|guṇ'|â-
vadyāni padyāni naḥ.
kasy' âsmiñ chatake sad|ambu|katake
doṣa|śrutiṃ kṣāmyati
niṣ|pratyūha|Vṛṣ'|âdri|nirjhara|jharat|
kāra|cchalen' ôccalan
dīn'|ālambana|divya|dampati|dayā|
kallola|kolāhalaḥ?

Fine. Let's assume that my poetry is a mix
of flaws and fine effects, all jumbled together.
Still, these Hundred Verses on Compassion
are the soap-nut that turns turbid water
clear. And even if someone points
to a flaw, who will hear him?
His voice will be drowned out
by the roaring torrents of inescapable
Compassion for all in need, gushing up
in the godly couple and washing over
Bull Hill.

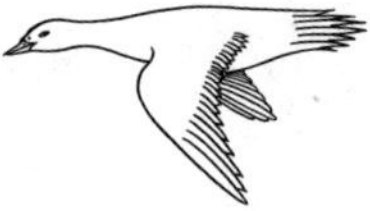

SELF-SURRENDER

1 KAS TE BODDHUM prabhavati paraṃ,
deva|deva, prabhāvaṃ,
yasmād itthaṃ vividha|racanā
sṛṣṭir eṣā babhūva?
bhakti|grāhyas tvam iha. tad api
tvām ahaṃ bhakti|mātrāt
stotuṃ vāñchāmy. atimahad idaṃ
sāhasaṃ me sahasva.

kṣity|ādīnām avayavavatāṃ
niścitaṃ janma tāvat.
tan n' âsty eva kva cana kalitaṃ
kartṛ|adhiṣṭhāna|hīnam.
n' âdhiṣṭhātuṃ prabhavati jaḍo
n' âpy an|īśaś ca bhāvas.
tasmād ādyas tvam asi jagatāṃ,
nātha, jāne, vidhātā.

Indraṃ Mitraṃ Varuṇam Anilaṃ
Padmajaṃ Viṣṇum Īśaṃ
prāhus te te, parama|Śiva, te
māyayā mohitās tvām.
etaiḥ sārdhaṃ sakalam api yac
chakti|leśe samāptaṃ,
sa tvaṃ devaḥ śrutiṣu viditaḥ
Śambhur ity ādi|devaḥ.

IS THERE ANYONE who could fathom 1
your depth, god of gods?
All of creation, with all its colors
and shades, comes from there.
That being said, they also say
that you can be grasped
through love. So through love
and love only, I want to sing
of you. You'll just have to put up with
my monumental folly.

One thing is for sure: complex entities,
made up of earth and other elements,
have a beginning. And what's more,
it's unthinkable that what has a beginning
has no creator. Furthermore, nothing that is not alive
could be that Creator—nothing
that is not God. Ergo, in my humble opinion,
it must be you, Lord,
who designed this vivid world.

Indra, Mitra, Váruna, Agni,
Brahma, Vishnu, Isha—these are some of the names
they use for you, Shiva the Supreme,
when dazzled by your tricks.
But all of them, and everything else too,
add up to no more than the tiniest fraction
of what you can be. You're Shambhu,
God of the Beginning,
what the Vedas are all about.

ānand'|âbdheḥ kam api ca ghanī|
bhāvam āsthāya rūpaṃ
śaktyā sārdhaṃ paramam Umayā
śāśvataṃ bhogam icchan
adhv'|âtīte, śuci|divasakṛt|
koṭi|dīpre, Kapardin,
ādye sthāne viharasi sadā
sevyamāno gaṇ'|ēśaiḥ.

5 tvaṃ Vedāntair vividha|mahimā
gīyase, viśva|netas.
tvaṃ vipr'|ādyair, vara|da, nikhilair
ijyase karmabhiḥ svaiḥ.
tvaṃ dṛṣṭ'|ânuśravika|viṣay'|ā-
nanda|mātrā|vitṛṣṇair
antar|granthi|pravilaya|kṛte
cintyase yogi|vṛndaiḥ.

dhyāyantas tvāṃ kati cana bhavaṃ
dus|taraṃ nistaranti,
tvat|pād'|âbjaṃ vidhivad itare
nityam ārādhayantaḥ,
anye varṇ'|āśrama|vidhi|ratāḥ,
pālayantas tvad|ājñāṃ.

First comes a certain thickening
into form, from out of endless joy.
Then all you want is to keep on tasting
the sweetness of your Shakti, Uma
the Supreme. So you take your stand
on this first place, to which there is no way,
lit by ten million suns and moons,
and play your game, long-haired god,
with your wild gang
for company.

When the Upanishads sing of that principle 5
that molds the world, they sing of you.
When Brahmins and others perform their rituals,
they offer all of them to you.
And as for the millions of yogis who've lost their taste
for even the tiniest shred of that happiness
that comes from looking and listening—
when they meditate to dissolve
the knots inside, they meditate
on you.

There are those who, by holding you
in their minds, cross over this uncrossable
sea. Others go by the book—
holding fast to your feet.
Then there are those who are enamored
of the conventions of caste and the rules
of when and how. They, too, take their orders
from you. But not me. I dropped out.

sarvaṃ hitvā bhava|jala|nidhāv
  eṣa majjāmi ghore.

utpady' âpi, Smara|hara, mahaty
  uttamānāṃ kule 'sminn,
 āsvādya tvan|mahima|jaladher
  apy ahaṃ śīkar'|âṇūn,
tvat|pād'|ârcā|vimukha|hṛdayaś
  cāpalād indriyāṇāṃ
 vyagras tuccheṣv, ahaha, jananaṃ
  vyarthayāmy eṣa pāpaḥ.

arka|droṇa|prabhṛti|kusumair
  arcanaṃ te vidheyaṃ.
 prāpyaṃ tena, Smara|hara,
  phalaṃ mokṣa|sāmrājya|lakṣmīḥ.
etaj jānann api, Śiva Śiva,
  vyarthayan kālam, ātmann,
 ātma|drohī karaṇa|vivaśo
  bhūyas" âdhaḥ patāmi.

kiṃ vā kurve viṣama|viṣaya|
  svairiṇā vairin' âhaṃ
 baddhaḥ, svāmin, vapuṣi
  hṛdaya|granthinā sārdham asmin?
ukṣṇā darpa|jvara|bhara|juṣā
  sākam ekatra naddhaḥ
 śrāmyan vatsaḥ, Smara|hara, yuge
  dhāvatā kiṃ karotu?

I'm drowning in this deadly
whirl of life.

I was born, Burner of Passion,* in the very best
of families. I drank in the spray
of your sweetness. Still, my senses
carried me away and my heart turned back
from loving your feet. I gave myself
to trifles. Hell, I'm no good. I've wasted
this life.

It would have been enough if I gave you
a few flowers and fragrant herbs in worship.
By now, Slayer of Passion, I'd be sitting
on the golden throne of freedom.
It's not as if I didn't know it.
God only knows that I've wasted
my time. I'm a slave to my senses,
a traitor to my self, the Self
that is you. I can't keep myself
from falling.

What can I do? I'm locked
into this body together with
my enemy, my knotted heart
that roams at will in the wilderness
of its desires. I'm like a calf
yoked together with a racing bull,
wild with pride. All I can do,
Burner of Passion,
is to keep on running.

n' âhaṃ roddhuṃ karaṇa|nicayaṃ
dur|nayaṃ pārayāmi.
smāraṃ smāraṃ jani|patha|rujaṃ,
nātha, sīdāmi bhītyā.
kiṃ vā kurve? kim ucitam iha?
kv' âdya gacchāmi? hanta,
tvat|pād'|âbja|prapadanam ṛte
n' âiva paśyāmy upāyam.

ullaṅghy' ājñām, uḍu|pati|kalā|
cūḍa, te, viśva|vandya,†
tyakt'|ācāraḥ paśuvad adhunā
mukta|lajjaś† carāmi.
evaṃ nānā|vidha|bhava|tati|
prāpta|dīrgh'|âparādhaḥ
kleś'|âmbhodhiṃ katham aham ṛte
tvat|prasādāt tareyam?

kṣāmyasy eva tvam iha karuṇā|
sāgaraḥ kṛtsnam āgaḥ
saṃsār'|ôtthaṃ, Giriśa, sa|bhaya|
prārthanā|dainya|mātrāt.
ady' âpy† evaṃ pratikalam ahaṃ

11 *viśvavandya* ASed : *viśvavandyāṃ* ASalt 11 *muktalajjaś* ASalt : *muktalajjaiś* ASed 12 *adyāpy* ASalt : *yady apy* ASed

I can't manage this unruly
squadron of my senses.
The more I think about it—
about this disease of life
after life—fear gets me down.
What can I do?
What should I do?
Where can I go?
Damn it, I see no other way
but to throw myself
at your feet.

I break all your rules,
god crowned by a sliver of the moon,
god whom everyone else obeys.
I've shown decency the door. Now
I lead my brazen life, more animal
than man. I have a long, impressive
record of misdeeds, from life after life.
How can I cross this sea of misery
unless you choose
to help me?

Since your mercy is deep as the ocean,
won't you please put up
with the whole package of my crimes,
the natural product of being alive?
Do it, God, out of pity, when you hear
my fearful plea. I'll keep on begging,
without shame, even as I pile on new crimes,

vyaktam āgaḥ|sahasraṃ
kurvan mūkaḥ† katham iva tathā
nistrapaḥ prārthayeyam?

sarvaṃ kṣeptuṃ† prabhavati janaḥ
saṃsṛti|prāptam āgaś
cetaḥ śvāsa|praśama|samaye
tvat|pad'|âbje nidhāya.
tasmin kāle yadi mama mano,
nātha, doṣa|tray'|ârtaṃ
prajñā|hīnaṃ, Purahara, bhavet,
tat kathaṃ me ghaṭeta?

prāṇ'|ôtkrānti|vyatikara|dalat|
saṃdhi|bandhe śarīre
prem'|āveśa|prasarad|amit'|ā-
krandite bandhu|varge
antaḥ|prajñām api, Śiva, bhajann
antarāyair an|antair
āviddho 'haṃ tvayi katham imām
arpayiśyāmi buddhim?

15 ady' âiva tvat|pada|nalinayor
arpayāmy, antar|ātmann,
ātmānaṃ me saha parikarair,
adri|kany"|âdhinātha.
n' âhaṃ boddhuṃ, Śiva, tava padaṃ,
na kriyā|yoga|caryāḥ

12 *mūkaḥ* ASed : *mūrkhaḥ* ASalt   13 *tarttuṃ* ASed : *tarttuṃ* ASalt

minute by minute, in broad daylight.
Do I have to spell out
the details?

They say that we can cast off
the whole burden of sin if, with our
last breath, we turn our thoughts
to your feet. But what if,
Lord, Burner of Cities,
at that very moment, when all
systems fail, I won't have
the presence of mind?*

When my breath leaves me behind,
and all goes slack that holds this body together,
and while my dear ones, overcome by love,
burst into wailing—let's suppose,
Shiva, that at that moment, against all odds,
I'll somehow hold on to awareness.
Still, I'll be dead
before I have a chance to offer you
my mind.

Now is the time.
I'm at your feet.
I take my self and offer it,
together with everyone around me,
to Myself,
that is, to You, Lord,
Lover of the Mountain's Daughter.
I'll never understand you, Shiva,

kartuṃ śaknomy; an|itara|gatiḥ
kevalaṃ tvāṃ prapadye.

yaḥ sraṣṭāraṃ nikhila|jagatāṃ
nirmame pūrvam īśas,
tasmai vedān adita sakalān
yaś ca sākaṃ purāṇaiḥ,
taṃ tvām ādyaṃ gurum aham asāv
ātma|buddhi|prakāśaṃ
saṃsār'|ārtaḥ śaraṇam adhunā
Pārvat"|īśaṃ prapadye.

Brahm'|ādīn yaḥ, Smara|hara, paśūn
moha|pāśena baddhvā
sarvān ekaś cid|acid|adhikaḥ
kārayitv" ātma|kṛtyam,
yaś c' âiteṣu sva|pada|śaraṇān
vidyayā mocayitvā
sāndr'|ānandaṃ gamayati paraṃ
dhāma, taṃ tvāṃ prapadye.

and I'm far from being good at yoga,
rites, and prayers.
There is no other way.
I give myself
to you.

He's the one who first created
the creator of all worlds, and he's the one
who gave that creator all the Vedas
and other books of yore—
to Him, that is, You, first of all gurus,
shining Self in the mind,
this I, sick from the world, now comes
for refuge. I give myself
to Párvati's Lord.

He's the one who binds all beings
from the creator on down with the shackles
of confusion, and he alone,
bigger than the breathing and the dead,
makes them all do what they must do.
He's also the one who unties
those among them who seek true
knowledge at his feet, and who leads them
to his high home, made
of sheer happiness. I give my self
to him,
to you.

bhakt'|âgryāṇāṃ katham api parair
yo '|cikitsyām a|martyaiḥ
saṃsār'|ākhyāṃ śamayati rujaṃ
sv'|ātma|bodh'|āuṣadhena,
taṃ, sarv'|âdhīśvara Bhava, mahā|
dīrgha|tīvr'|āmayena
kliṣṭo 'haṃ tvāṃ, vara|da, śaraṇaṃ
yāmi saṃsāra|vaidyam.

dhyāto yatnād vijita†|karaṇair
yogibhir yo vimṛgyas†
tebhyāṃ prāṇ'|ôtkramaṇa|samaye
saṃnidhāy' ātman" âiva
tad vyācaṣṭe bhava|bhaya|haraṃ
tārakaṃ brahma|devas.
taṃ seve 'haṃ, Giriśa, satataṃ
brahma|vidyā|guruṃ tvām.

«dāso 'sm'» îti tvayi, Śiva, mayā
nitya|siddhaṃ nivedyaṃ.
jānāsy etat tvam api, yad ahaṃ
nir|gatiḥ saṃbhramāmi.
n' âsty ev' ânyan mama kim api te,
nātha, vijñāpanīyaṃ.
kāruṇyān me śaraṇa|varaṇaṃ
dīna|vṛtter gṛhāṇa.

---

19 *vijita* ASed : *niśita* ASalt   19 *vimṛgyas* ASed : *'vimukte* ASvl : *vimuktyai* ASvl : *vimuktais* ASvl

He's the one who can cure his devotees
of what no other god can cure, the incurable
disease called "life." The special drug he prescribes
is "Know Yourself." And since I've got a bad case
of this epidemic, with a long history of former bouts,
I've come to the one doctor whose specialty
is life. God of everything,
giver of boons—
I'm in trouble.
I've come to you.

Yogis who've conquered their senses
seek him in their meditation, and he comes to them,
himself, at the moment their breath departs
and whispers the secret mantra that carries them across,
the one that does away with fear, with his own lips.
Gírisha, master of secrets:
I'm your servant
forever.

Shiva, I'm your slave.
It's a well-known fact.
You also know how I live
my life, roaming aimlessly,
with no other place to go.
Is there anything else you need to know
about me? Say yes to the plea
of this all-too-miserable creature.
Do it
out of pity.

Brahm'|Ôpendra|prabhṛtibhir api
sv'|ēpsita|prārthanāya,
svāminn, agre ciram avasaras
toṣayadbhiḥ pratīkṣyaḥ.
drāg eva tvāṃ yad iha śaraṇaṃ
prārthaye kīṭa|kalpas,
tad, viśv'|âdhīśvara, tava kṛpām
eva viśvasya dīne.

karma|jñāna|pracayam akhilaṃ
duṣ|karaṃ, nātha, paśyan,
pāp'|āsaktaṃ hṛdayam api c' â|
pārayan saṃnirodhum,
saṃsār'|ākhye, Purahara, mahaty andha|kūpe viṣīdan
hast'|ālamba|prapatanam† idaṃ
prāpya te nir|bhayo 'smi.

tvām ev' âikaṃ hata|jani|pathe
pāntham asmin prapañce
matvā janma|pralaya|jaladher
bibhyataḥ pāra|śūnyāt
yat te dhanyāḥ, sura|vara, mukhaṃ
dakṣiṇaṃ saṃśrayanti,
kliṣṭaṃ ghore ciram iha bhave
tena māṃ pāhi nityam.

22 *prapatanam* ASed : *prapadanam* ASalt

The high and mighty gods—
Brahma the creator, Vishnu, you name them—
they've been waiting a long long time,
singing your praises at your doorstep,
hoping you'll give them
what they want. I, on the other hand,
no better than a worm, expect you to answer
my prayers right away. I'm truly wretched
and I know I can count
on your kindness.

I can see that the whole business
of performing rituals and finding truth
is just too much for me. Nor do I stand a chance
of keeping my heart from its favorite misdeeds.
But even though I'm stuck in this deep dark
pit called "life," Burner of Cities,
I'm not afraid. I know you'll stretch out your hand
to throw me a rope.*

A few lucky souls sense that on the doomed path
of living in this world, they're lost
without you. They know that they're drowning
in the ocean of birth and death that has
no shore. So they cast their hopes
on a welcoming smile from you,
first among gods.
But what about me? I've been suffering
for what seems like forever—the same
dreadful deal. Won't you smile at me, too,
once and for all?*

eko 'si tvaṃ, Śiva, janimatām
īśvaro bandha|muktyoḥ.
kleś'|âṅgār'|âvaliṣu luṭhataḥ
kā gatis tvāṃ vinā me?
tasmād asminn iha, Paśupate,
ghora|janma|pravāhe
khinnaṃ dainy'|ākaram ati|bhayaṃ
māṃ bhajasva prapannam.

25 yo devānāṃ prathamam a|śubha|
drāvako bhakti|bhājāṃ,
pūrvaṃ, viśv'|âdhika, Śata|dhṛtiṃ
jāyamānaṃ maha"|rṣiḥ
dṛṣṭy"|âpaśyat sakala|jagatī|
sṛṣṭi|sāmarthya|dātryā,
sa tvaṃ granthi|pravilaya|kṛte
vidyayā yojay' âsmān.

yady ākāśaṃ, śubha|da, manujāś
carmavad veṣṭayeyur,
duḥkhasy' ântaṃ tad api puruṣas
tvām a|vijñāya n' âiti.
vijñānaṃ ca tvayi, Śiva, ṛte
tvat|prasādān na labhyaṃ.
tad duḥkh'|ārtaḥ kam iha śaraṇaṃ
yāmi devaṃ tvad|anyam?

For everyone alive, you, alone, are the lock
and key. Turning and turning in this fiery
gyre, I've no way out but you. I'm adrift,
swept through terrible birth
after birth. A mine
of misery. Scared to death.
I surrender, Shiva,
Lord of Beasts.
Stay with me.

You're the one who melts down the dross
of our deeds. And you're the one who turned
your gaze toward Brahma, born first of all gods,
to instill him with the gift of creating
our world. Couldn't you tie us to the yoke
of knowledge, so we can untie
our knots?

Even if people were to cloak themselves
in thin air, or if the sky were their skin,
not even one person would ever
reach the end of suffering without
knowing you. But no one can know
you, Shiva, giver of good,
unless you let yourself
be known. So here I am,
still suffering. What god can I turn to
but you?

kiṃ gūḍh'|ârthair a|kṛtaka|vaco|
gumphanaiḥ, kiṃ purāṇais,
tantr'|ādyair vā puruṣa|matibhir
dur|nirūpy'|âika|matyaiḥ?
kiṃ vā śāstrair a|phala|kalah'|ôl-
lāsa|mātra|pradhānair?
vidyā, vidy"|ēśvara, kṛta|dhiyāṃ
kevalaṃ tvat|prasādāt.

pāpiṣṭho 'haṃ, viṣaya|capalaḥ,
saṃtata|droha|śālī,
kārpaṇy'|âika|sthira|nivasatiḥ,
puṇya|gandh'|ân|abhijñaḥ.
yady apy evaṃ, tad api, śaraṇa,
tvat|pad'|âbjaṃ prapannaṃ
n' âinaṃ dīnaṃ, Smara|hara, tav' ô-
pekṣituṃ, nātha, yuktam.

ālocy' âivaṃ mayi yadi bhavān,
nātha, doṣān an|antān
asmat|pād'|āśrayaṇa|padavīṃ
n' âhat' îti kṣipen mām,
ady' âiv' êmaṃ śaraṇa|viharād
viddhi bhīty" âiva naṣṭaṃ.
grāmo gṛhṇāty a|hita|tanayaṃ
kiṃ nu mātrā nirastam?

Who needs all the cryptic scriptures
that no man has made, or the old books,
or the tantric treatises, so abstruse
that no two human minds would ever agree
on what they mean? And who needs the scientific
screeds, so full of futile strife and nothing more?
Real knowledge, god of knowledge,
is yours to give to anyone
who makes up
his mind.

Just look at me: I'm the worst ever.
A slave to caprice. A specialist in long-term
treachery. A permanent resident in the realm
of misery. I've never had a whiff of what it feels like
to be kind. Nonetheless, god of shelter,
Burner of Passion,
it doesn't seem right for you to ignore
this wretched person who's fallen
at your feet.

If, lord, after reckoning up the infinity
of my flaws, you cut me off as unworthy
of falling at your feet, then you should know:
I'm scared to death, I'm crushed by the thought
that now I've nowhere to go. Who would take in
a wicked child disowned
by his own mother?

kṣantavyaṃ vā nikhilam api me
bhūta|bhāvi vyalīkaṃ,
dur|vyāpāra|pravaṇam atha vā
śikṣaṇīyaṃ mano me.
na tv ev' ārtyā nir|atiśayayā
tvat|pad'|âbjam prapannaṃ
tvad|vinyast'|âkhila|bharam amuṃ
yuktam, īśa, prahātum.

sarvajñas tvaṃ, nir|avadhi|kṛpā|
sāgaraḥ, puṇya|śaktiḥ,
kasmād enaṃ na gaṇayasi māṃ
āpad|abdhau nimagnam?
ekaṃ pāp'|ātmakam api rujā
sarvato 'tyanta|dīnaṃ
jantuṃ yady uddharasi, Śiva, kas
tāvat" âti|prasaṅgaḥ?

«atyant'|ârti|vyathitam a|gatiṃ,
deva, mām uddhar',» êti
kṣuṇṇo mārgas tava bata purā
kena vā, nātha|nātha?
kām ālambe bata tad|adhikāṃ
prārthanā|rītim anyāṃ?
trāyasv' âinaṃ sapadi kṛpayā
vastu|tattvaṃ vicintya.

Or maybe just forgive everything
I've done wrong, and all future wrongs,
while you're at it. Another option
is to take this mind, so perverse
in its ways, and fix it. What you can't do,
God, now that I've come to you in unrivaled
distress and unloaded my whole burden
at your feet, is
to leave me.

You know it all. Your mercy knows
no boundary. You're brimming with power.
Why can't you think of me, drowning
in disaster. Let's say, Shiva, you rescue
one creature who is wicked to the bone, sick
as sick can be. Would that be too much
to ask?

I don't know if anyone has traveled this path
before me—if anyone has asked you to rescue
someone wretched to the bone. Someone hopeless
like me. What option do I have left?
I can only beg you to think things over
kindly and to save me
now.

etāvantaṃ bhramaṇa|nicayaṃ
prāpito 'yaṃ varākaḥ.
śrāntaḥ, svāminn, a|gatir adhunā
mocanīyas tvay" âham.
kṛty'|â|kṛtya|vyapagata|matir
dīna|śākhā|mṛgo 'yaṃ.
saṃtāḍy' âinaṃ daśana|vivṛtiṃ
paśyatas te phalaṃ kim?

«mātā,» «tātaḥ,» «suta,» iti samā—
badhya māṃ moha|pāśair
āpāty' âivaṃ bhava|jala|nidhau,
hā, kiṃ, īśa, tvay" âptam?
etāvantaṃ samayam iyatīm
ārtim āpādite 'smin
kalyāṇī te kim iti na kṛpā?
k" âpi me bhāgya|rekhā?

bhuṅkṣe guptaṃ bata sukha|nidhiṃ,
tāta, sādhāraṇaṃ tvaṃ
bhikṣā|vṛttiṃ param abhinayan
māyayā māṃ vibhajya.
maryādāyāḥ sakala|jagatāṃ
nāyakaḥ sthāpakas tvaṃ.
yuktaṃ kiṃ? tad vada vibhajanaṃ.
yojaya sv'|ātmanā mām.

This lowly fool has had his fill of wandering
from womb to womb. I'm tired, Lord,
and hopeless. You ought to free me now.
What do you get from beating up on this
poor monkey who's lost the knack
of knowing right from wrong?
Do you get a kick from watching him
bare his teeth?

"Mother," "father," "son"—you've tied me up
in all these knots of delusion and dumped me
in the sea of births. What the hell
did you get out of it? I've been in agony
for so long. Have you run out
of kindness? Isn't there even one lucky line
on my palm?

You play the beggar's role to perfection,
but really, Father, you're eating up in secret
our common store of pleasures, depriving me
of my rightful share. You're the leader
of all worlds. You set the boundaries. Tell me,
is this a fair allocation? Give me back
myself and we'll be partners
again.

«na tvā janma|pracaya|jaladher
uddharām'» īti ced dhīr,
āstāṃ. tan me bhavatu ca janir
yatra kutr' âpi jātau.
tvad|bhaktānām an|itara|sukhaiḥ
pāda|dhūlī|kiśorair
ārabdhaṃ† me bhavatu, bhagavan,
bhāvi sarvaṃ śarīram.

kīṭā, nāgās, tarava iti vā
kiṃ na santi sthaleṣu
tvat|pād'|âmbhoruha|parimal'|ôd-
vāhi|mand'|ânileṣu?
teṣv ekaṃ vā sṛja punar imaṃ,
nātha dīn'|ārti|hārin,
ā toṣān māṃ mṛḍa bhava|mah"|âṅ-
gāra|nadyāṃ luṭhantam.

kāle kaṇṭha|sphurad|asu|kalā|
leśa|satt"|âvaloka|
vyagr'|ôdagra|vyasana|rudita†|
snigdha|ruddh'|ôpakaṇṭhe
antas|todair avadhi|rahitām
ārtim āpadyamāne 'py
aṅghri|dvandve tava niviśatām,
antar|ātman, mam' ātmā.

---

36 *ārabdhaṃ* ASed : *āliptaṃ* ASalt 38 *vyasanarudita* ASalt : *vyasani-sakala* ASed

Suppose you decide not to fish me out
of the sea of births. Fine. Let me be born
somewhere or other, as someone
or something. I don't care. Just make sure
that you make my next body out of particles
of dust from under the feet of your faithful
and nothing else. There's nothing
I want more.

Worms, snakes, trees—don't such things
exist in places where your fragrance is spread
by the soft southern wind? So just create me as
        one of them,
in some such place, as many times as you want.
You relieve the sorrows of all who suffer, Shiva,
and I—I'm swirling in the river of burning coals
they call life.

Death is here. Watching what's left of my life—
my last breaths, fluttering in my throat—
my loved ones, wailing, terrified
that the end has come, close in on me,
while within I suffer endlessly,
blow after blow. Now, even now,
I pray to Myself, who is you,
to let my self come to rest
at your feet.

antar|bāṣp'|ākulita|nayanān
antar|aṅgān a|paśyan,
agre ghoṣaṃ rudita|bahulaṃ
kātarāṇām a|śṛṇvan,
aty|utkrānti|śramam a|gaṇayann
anta|kāle, Kapardin,
anghri|dvaṃdve tava niviśatām,
antar|ātman, mam' ātmā.

cāru|smer'|ānana|sarasijaṃ
candra|rekh''|âvataṃsaṃ
phullan|mallī|kusuma|kalikā|
dāma|saubhāgya|coram
antaḥ paśyāmy a|cala|sutayā
ratna|pīṭhe niṣaṇṇaṃ,
lok'|âtītaṃ, satata|śiva|daṃ
rūpam a|prākṛtaṃ te.

svapne v'' âpi sva|rasa|vikasad|
divya|paṅkeruh'|ābhaṃ
paśyeyaṃ kiṃ tava, Paśupate,
pāda|yugmaṃ kadā cit?
kv' âhaṃ pāpaḥ, kva tava caraṇ'|ā-
loka|bhāgyaṃ? tath'' âpi
pratyāśāṃ me ghaṭayati punar
viśrutā te 'nukampā.

Let it not see my dear ones, their eyes drowning
in tears. Let it not hear all the commotion,
the weeping of those filled with fear.
Let it pay no heed, Lord of long, matted hair,
to the agony of departing when time comes
to an end. I pray to Myself, who is you,
to let my self come to rest
at your feet.

I look inside, and what I see is a lotus opening
in a smile, a crown made from a sliver
of the moon, a thief who made off with the fresh charm
of jasmine buds strung together, unfolding.
You sit there on a throne of jewels together
with the Mountain's Daughter, your body
beautiful beyond anything in this world
and made of nothing we can know,
that gives the endless blessing
that is Shiva.

Will I ever, even in a dream, see your feet—
a peerless pair of lotuses freely bursting
with honey? What chance do the eyes
of an outlaw like me stand of winning
such a prize? My only hope,
Lord of Beasts,
is that you'll live up to your reputation
for compassion.

bhikṣā|vṛttiṃ cara, pitṛ|vane
bhūta|saṅghair bhram'—êdaṃ
vijñātaṃ te caritam akhilaṃ
vipralipsoḥ, Kapālin.
ā|Vaikuṇṭha|Druhiṇam akhila|
prāṇinām īśvaras tvaṃ,
nātha. svapne 'py aham iha na te
pāda|padmaṃ tyajāmi.

ālepanaṃ bhasitam, āvasathaḥ śmaśānam,
asthīni te satatam ābharaṇāni santu.
nihnotum, īśa, sakala|śruti|pāra|siddham
aiśvaryam Ambujabhavo 'pi ca na kṣamas te.

vividham api guṇ'|âughaṃ vedayantv artha|vādāḥ
parimita|vibhavānāṃ pāmarāṇāṃ surāṇām.
tanu|himakara|maule, tāvatā tvatparatve
kati kati jagad|īśāḥ kalpitā no bhaveyuḥ.

vihara pitṛ|vane vā, viśva|pāre pure vā,
rajata|giri|taṭe vā, ratna|sānu|sthale vā,
diśa bhavad|upakaṇṭhaṃ. dehi me bhṛtya|bhāvaṃ,
parama|Śiva, tava śrī|pāduk'|āvāhakānām.

Carry on with your begging from door
to door. Hang out with your ghoulish
buddies in the burning grounds.
I know your whole history of deceit,
long-haired god, I know you're really lord
of Vishnu and Brahma and everything
alive. From now on I'll never let go,
even in my sleep, of your
two lotus feet.

For sandal paste—burnt ash.
Your home address—the cremation grounds.
Ornaments—bones and more bones.
But, lord, your commanding power,
affirmed at the limit of all the Vedas—
not even the Creator himself
can disguise it.

Let the Vedas babble on about the fancy
fortes of petty gods with their feeble
claims to fame. As we know the vastness
of your might, god crowned
with the slender moon, we can afford
to dream up as many good gods
as we like.

Roam the burning grounds 45
or the highest city,
or the silvery slopes of Kailása,
or the jewel-studded peaks of Mount Meru.
Wherever you are, lead me there, Shiva.

balam a|balam amīṣāṃ balbajānāṃ vicintyaṃ
katham api, Śiva, kāla|kṣepa|mātra|pradhānaiḥ
nikhilam api rahasyaṃ, nātha, niṣkṛṣya sākṣāt
Sarasijabhava|mukhyaiḥ sādhitaṃ naḥ pramāṇam.

na kiṃ cin mene 'taḥ
samabhilaṣaṇīyaṃ tri|bhuvane.
sukhaṃ vā duḥkhaṃ vā—
mama bhavatu yad bhāvi, bhagavan.
samunmīlat|pātho|
ruha|kuhara|saubhāgya|muṣi te
pada|dvaṃdve cetaḥ
paricayam upeyān mama sadā.

udara|bharaṇa|mātraṃ sādhyam uddiśya nīceṣv
a|sakṛd|upanibaddhām, āhit'|ôcchiṣṭa|bhāvām,
aham iha nuti|bhaṅgīm arpayitv" ôpahāraṃ,
tava caraṇa|saroje, tāta, jāto 'parādhī.

sarvaṃ, sadā|Śiva, sahasva mam' âparādhaṃ.
magnaṃ samuddhara mahaty amum āpad|abdhau.
sarv'|ātmanā tava pad'|âmbujam eva dīnaḥ,
svāminn, an|anya|śaraṇaḥ śaraṇaṃ prapadye.

Let me be the slave of those who bear
your sandals.

Let those keen on wasting time
ponder the points weak and strong
of these men of straw. If Brahma
and the other goods have managed to unearth
the secret, Shiva, and keep it whole
in their minds, that's all the proof
we need.

I can't think of anything else in the world
to wish for. Come happiness, come pain—
whatever will be, lord, let it be.
Your two feet have stolen
the soft splendor from inside the lotus
as it unfolds: I want my mind
to be their friend
forever.

Seeing no farther than my next meal,
I've offered you this praise of sorts:
made of words for lowly things, chewed up,
spit out, and recycled. What a mistake!
What a gift to give a father!*

You must forgive, eternal Shiva,
every mistake of mine. You must rescue
this drowning man from the vast ocean
of disaster. I'm desperate, Master,
I've no other shelter.

50 Ātm'|ârpaṇa|stutir iyaṃ, bhagavan, nibaddhā
yady apy an|anya|manasā na mayā, tath" âpi
«vāc" âpi kevalam ayaṃ śaraṇaṃ vṛṇīte
dīno varāka,» iti rakṣa, kṛpā|nidhe, mām.

I give myself with all my self
to your lotus-like feet,
my one refuge.

So much for "Self-Surrender."
It's not as if I composed it
with a focused mind. Still,
just say to yourself:
"This poor excuse for a man
is only asking for shelter,
muttering mere words."
God rich in compassion:
please look after me.

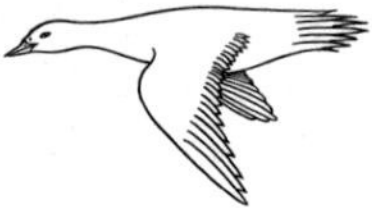

PEACE

1 VAṂŚE KASMINN ajaniṣi? kayoḥ
putratām agrahīṣam?
katy aśrauṣam—tad api katidhā,
tac ca sadbhyaḥ katibhyaḥ?
kiṃ n' âdrākṣaṃ vyasanam? api vā
kiṃ sukhaṃ n' ânvabhūvaṃ?
n' ôpāraṃsīt tad api hṛdayaṃ.
kīdṛśo me vipākaḥ?

pādau me staḥ parama|caturau
kīkaṭān eva gantuṃ.
vāg apy āste nibhṛtam an|ṛtāny
eva vaktuṃ vacāṃsi.
mīmāṃsante mama ca matayo
doṣa|dṛṣṭau pareṣāṃ.
paṅgur mūkaḥ paśur api bhavāmy
ātmanīne tu kṛtye.

yām ārāddhuṃ na gaṇitam idaṃ
jīvitaṃ vā dhanaṃ vā,
yasyāḥ prītir manasi kalitā
jyāyasī mokṣato 'pi.
s" âiv' êdānīṃ vayasi calite
saṃprahīṇe ca vitte
tūlāy' âpi, Tripurahara, māṃ
manyate n' âiva bhāryā.

WHAT A FAMILY to be born into! Can you believe 1
who turned out to be my parents?
And all the lectures I've heard—the finest professors,
the range of topics, class after class…
I've seen how bad the world can be. Tasted
every pleasure. What I've never managed
is a quiet heart. As you can see,
I've got it made.

My feet always know the way straight
to the crooked alleys.
My tongue follows its secret agenda:
to tell lies and lies alone.
My clever mind searches out the finest faults
in everyone. But when it comes to doing
what's good for me, I'm a lame
dumb beast.

To make her happy, I didn't think twice
about throwing away my wealth or my life.
Her love was dearer to my heart
than the rapture of release.
And now that my life is spent,
and my money too, my dear wife
thinks less of me, Shiva,
Burner of Cities,
than a ball of fluff.

kṛtvā pāpāny api khalu mayā
posịtāḥ śaiśave ye,
nidr"|āhārāv api vijahatā
śiksịtā ye kalāsu,
prādur|bhūtāḥ svayam iva hi te,
prāktan'|â|dṛṣṭa|labdha|
prajñ"|ônmeṣā iva ca tanayā
na smaranty ātmano 'pi.

dārāḥ, putrāḥ, parama|suhṛdo,
bāndhavāḥ, kiṃkarā vā
svapn'|âvasthāsv api ca virahaṃ
ye mayā na kṣamante,
aty|āsanne tapana|tanayasy'
ājñayā dūta|varge
teṣv eko 'pi, Smara|hara, na me
gantum anvasti jantuḥ.

rājño bhṛtyā yadi paricitā,
deśikasy' âiṣa lābho.
rāja|dvāre yadi khalu gataṃ,
Naimiśe tat praviṣṭam.
rājā dṛṣṭo 'tha ca yadi, paraṃ
Brahma sākṣāt|kṛtaṃ tat.

When they were little,
I would have killed
to provide for them.
I didn't sleep, I didn't eat,
but I put them through school.
Now these children of mine
think they were born out of thin air,
bringing with them great wisdom
from a previous life.
They don't remember
who they are.

My wife, my sons, closest friends,
my relatives, servants, whoever—
can't bear to part from me
even in their dreams.
But when the horde of Death's messengers
come knocking on my door,
not even one of them, Shiva,
Killer of Passion,*
will volunteer to join me.

If you have the great good fortune,
of making friends with the king's close aides,
you've found your guru.
If they let you past the gate,
you're in heaven.
Then, if you get to meet the king in person,
it'll be like shaking God's hand.
And if you drop dead at your post in the palace,
as far as I'm concerned,

tyakto deho yadi nṛpa|kule,
mādṛśāṃ so 'pavargaḥ.

yat tīrthānām aṭanam atha, yat
pūjanaṃ devatānām,
iṣṭ'|āpūrta|vyasanam api yad,
yac ca dākṣyaṃ kalāsu—
artha|prāpty|aupayikam akhilaṃ
jāyate mādṛśāṃ tat.
te c' âpy arthā dharaṇi|śaraṇā,
bhūmibhṛtsāt kṛtā vā.

ā kaumārād guru|caraṇa|śu-
śrūṣayā brahma|vidyāsv
āsthāy' āsthām, ahaha, mahatīm
ārjitaṃ kauśalaṃ yat,
nidrā|hetor niśi niśi kathāḥ
śṛṇvatāṃ pārthivānāṃ
kāla|kṣep'|âupayikam idam apy,
āḥ, kathaṃ paryaṇaṃsīt?

chāyā, toyaṃ, vasanam, aśanaṃ,
vāhanaṃ, dīpikā vā
kretuṃ yasmin kila na su|labhaṃ
kiṃ cid apy eṣu martyaiḥ,
tasmin dūre pathi tanu|bhṛtāṃ
sarvath" âiv' âbhigamye

that's instant
redemption.

Pilgrimage to holy places,
worshiping the gods,
an obsession with rituals and charity,
mastery of the arts—
for people like me,
all these are only
ways of getting rich.
And then what happens?
We either bury the money in the ground
or surrender it to the king.

All the trouble I took,
ever since I was a kid
serving at the feet of my teachers,
to fathom the secrets of God—
look what came out of it:
the stuff of bedtime stories
that I tell yawning kings,
night after night,
to kill time.

Shade, water, clothing, food,
transportation, light—
where we mortals have to go,
not one of them is for sale.
It's a long road, and the journey
must begin with a certain something

prasthān'|ârhaṃ kam api tu vidhiṃ
ghasmarā na smarāmaḥ.

ākarṇyante tapana|tanaya|
grāma|saṃlāpa|ghoṣā.
mandaṃ mandaṃ hrasati nihitaḥ
kāla|pāśo 'pi kaṇṭhe.
āpṛcchyante kṛta|jigamiṣā|
saṃbhramāḥ prāṇa|vātāḥ.
n' âiv' êdānīm api viṣaya|vai-
mukhyam abhyeti cetaḥ.

cakṣuṣy andhe, calati daśane,
śmaśruṇi śvetamāne,
sīdaty aṅge, manasi kaluṣe,
kampamāne kar'|âgre,
dūtair etair Dinakarabhuvaḥ
śaśvad udbodhyamānās
trātuṃ dehaṃ tad api bhiṣajām
eva sāntvaṃ vadāmaḥ.

śānto vahnir jaṭhara|piṭhare.
saṃsthitā kāma|vārtā.
dhāvaṃ dhāvaṃ diśi diśi śanair

that we, in our body's hunger,
can't seem to remember.*

I can hear them coming—
the whole loud bunch, Death's deafening
delegation. Slowly but surely,
his noose around my neck
is getting tighter.
My very breath, itching to move on,
has come to say goodbye.
And even now my heart grabs
at whatever it desires
and won't let go.

My eyes have gone blind,
my teeth are gone altogether,
my moustache has turned white,
my body's giving out,
my mind is not clear,
my fingers tremble.
These telltale messengers of Death
keep trying to wake me up,
but I know my body
is in good hands. I go on
chanting the doctors'
soothing incantation.

The fire that was burning in my gut
has flickered out.
My love life
is a faded rumor.

indriy'|âśvā nipetuḥ.
evaṃ daivād uparamam agād
eṣa me vairi|vargaś.
cetas tv ekaṃ na vaśam ayate.
kiṃ karomi? kva yāmi?

nān" ôpāyair diśi diśi dhanāny
arjayitvā, vyayitvā,
samyak saṃpāditam idam, aho,
sthaulyam ekaṃ śarīre.
śrutvā śrutvā bahu|jana|mukhād
āyuṣ" âitāvat" âpi
prāptaṃ darś'|âvadhi|timiravad
gāḍham a|jñānam ekam.

kv' ēkṣante māṃ kva cana śayitaṃ
kiṃkarā Daṇḍapāṇer?
īkṣantāṃ vā, tad api mayi kiṃ
kuryur uddāma|vṛtte?
kuryuḥ kiṃ cit, prasabham api vā
ghātayiṣyāmi rājñ"—êty
antar|dhairyaṃ param iha vahann
Antakaṃ na smarāmi.

The wild horses that were my senses
shot off in all directions and then
dropped dead, one by one.
As you can see, fate has struck down
all the enemies I had.
Only my heart is left,
and it won't give up.
What now?
Where to?

Here and there, by hook
or by crook, I made a lot of money.
Spent some too. Now all I have
to show for it is my big potbelly.
People gave me good advice, over and over,
all through my life. And what did I gain?
One fat lump of ignorance, dark
as a moonless night.

Death's messengers?
How will they ever find me,
lying in my hole?
Suppose they do find me,
what can they do?
They won't mess with me.
Suppose they do try something?
I'll put the king on their case
right away. I'm much too important
to think about dying.

15 Vedā vā syur vitatha|vacanā;
vismared Īśvaro vā
dharm'|â|dharma|sthiti|viracanām;
Antako vā mṛṣā syāt;
nityo vā syām aham—iti bahūn
ullikhantaḥ samādhīn
medo|vṛddhyā mudita|manasaḥ
sarvato nirvṛtāḥ smaḥ.

yāme yāme galati vapuṣaḥ
sraṃsate sandhi|bandhaḥ.
śvāse śvāse 'pi ca vicalati
kṣīyate dīrgham āyuḥ.
bhukte bhukte 'pi ca sukha|lave
lupyate puṇya|rāśiḥ.
kṛtye kṛtye nir|avadhi punar
vardhate pātakaṃ naḥ.

gantavyo 'dhvā sakala|dur|ava-
sthāna|saṃpāta|bhūmir.
gatvā dṛśyas tri|bhuvana|jan'|ā-
yuṣ|kal"|ântaḥ Kṛtāntaḥ.
dṛṣṭvā labhyā niraya|janitā
yātanā n'|âika|bhedā.

The scriptures got it all wrong. 15
Either that, or God will loose track
of my records, my good deeds
and bad. Or maybe death isn't for real.
Or at least *I* am immortal...
I'm so creative when it comes
to crafting helpful theories.
Well fed, in high spirits.
I've every reason
to be happy.

Hour by hour, my joints
are coming unstuck.
Breath by breath, this long life
is dwindling.
Bite by bite, I'm eating up
my stock of merit.
(The tiniest tidbit makes a dent.)
The one thing that keeps growing,
deed by deed, is my endless
store of vice.

The road we must travel is a fertile ground
for all sorts of misery.
Having traveled it, we see the Terminator,
who puts an end to the sliver of life
that anyone gets to live.
Having seen him, we go straight to hell,
with its many interesting torments.
Somehow this whole package slips

vismṛty' êdaṃ nikhilam api tu
vyartham āyur nayāmaḥ.

kāle kāle na kim upanataṃ
bhuñjate bhojya|jātaṃ?
gṛhṇanty ambho na kim? atha na kiṃ
saṃviśanti kṣapāsu?
puṣṇanti svān na kim u pṛthukān?
strīṣu kiṃ no ramante?
kṛty'|â|kṛtya|vyapagata|dhiyāṃ
kas tiraścāṃ ca bhedaḥ?

kṛcchrāl labdhaṃ dhanam api śat'|âṃś'|
âdhika|prāpti|lobhāt
patre kiñ cil likhitam upalabhy'
âiva sarvaṃ tyajāmaḥ.
śāstraiḥ siddhe bahu|śata|guṇ'|â-
dhikya|lābhe paratra
vyarth'|āśaṅkā|kaluṣa|manaso
n' ôtsṛjāmo 'rtha|leśam.

jīrṇe, rugṇe, vikala|karaṇe,
śatrubhir vā gṛhīte
svasmin ko 'rtho bhavati sukha|daḥ?
kaś ca kāma|prasaṅgaḥ?
mā bhūd etat sakalam atha vā.
sv'|āyuṣaḥ kiṃ pramāṇaṃ?

our mind, and we lead our life
to no end.

Everything edible they come across,
at any moment—don't they gobble it up?
Don't they drink water and go to bed
at night? Don't they bring up their kids?
Have sex with their wives?
So what's the big difference between animals
and us, who couldn't care less
if something's wrong
or right?

Our life's savings—all that hard work!—
we risk it all when we come across
some scrap of paper promising a profit
of one percent. But when it comes to the life
beyond, where the profits in store are
a thousand times more (so the scriptures
ensure), we're so obsessed with overspending
that we won't risk
a penny.

When I'm old, sick, losing
my mind, easy prey
for my enemies, will money
buy me happiness?
And as for my love life …
But then again, none of this
may happen. And who says
life is short?

niścity' âivaṃ durita|nicayaś
cīyate nir|viśaṅkaiḥ.

āyānty agre nanu tanu|bhavā
uttama'|rṇā iv' ême.
śayyā|lagnāḥ phaṇa|bhṛta iv' ā-
bhānti dārā idānīm.
kārā|geha|pratimam adhunā
mandiraṃ dṛśyate me—
tatra sthātuṃ prasajati mano
na kṣaṇaṃ na kṣaṇ'|ârdham.

jātaṃ jātaṃ, gatam api gataṃ
bālyato laulyato vā.
n' êtaḥ stheyaṃ kṣaṇam api gṛhe—
muñcataḥ ko muhūrtaḥ?
ity atyanta|vyavasita|dhiyo
niḥsaranto 'pi gehād
āvartante jhaṭ|iti rudatāṃ
sāntva|hetoḥ śiśūnām.

Now that that's been resolved,
we're all too happy to rack up
reckless deeds.

These sons of mine, my own
flesh and blood, come at me
like loan-sharks.
When I look at my wife,
who shares my bed,
I see a snake.
My own home now feels
like a prison cell—
I don't want to stay here
one more second, or even
half a second.

I may have been stupid,
I may have been wayward.
But what has come has come
and what's gone is gone.
I won't stay in this house
another moment—anytime
is a good time to go.
I've made up my mind.
I'm on my way out.
But hey, the children are crying
and back I go.

n' âiva brūmo vayam, «atithayo,
'bhyāgatā, bandhu|vargā,
dīn'|â|nāthāḥ, suhṛda iti ye,
teṣu kāryā day"» êti.
«yaṃ tvaṃ poṣyaṃ manasi kuruṣe
nityam ātmanam ekaṃ,
janmany asminn iva bibhṛhi taṃ
sarvad",» êty ullapāmaḥ.|

«ko nu Vyāsaḥ?» «ka iva sa Manuḥ?»
«ko nv asau Yājñavalkyo?»
yair udghuṣṭaṃ hitam a|sakṛd a-
smāsu pitr" êva putre,
paśyāmas tān nir|upadhi|kṛpā|
sāgarāṃl loka|bandhūn,
paśyāmo 'smān nir|avadhi|tamaḥ|
kṣmādharān brahma|bandhūn.

yat tāmisre Naraka|kuhare,
yad bahiś Cakravālād,
yat Pātāle, yad api dharaṇau
vārṣikīṣu kṣapāsu,
rūḍhaṃ gāḍhaṃ tama iti sama-
staṃ ca tac cintyamānaṃ
n' āsmāk'|ântaḥkaraṇa|tamaso
dāsa|bhāve 'pi yogyam.

We're not saying that when guests
come knocking at your door, or friends,
or hordes of relatives, or those with no place
else to go, you really ought to feel
compassion. All we're saying is that
you should take good care of that one, unfailing
Self of yours—you may need it
in some future life.

"Who was Vyasa?" "Who was Manu?"
"Who was that Yajna·valkya?"
They're the ones who told us loudly,
time and again, what's good for us,
like a father teaching a son.
Look at them—infinite oceans
of compassion, true friends
to the whole world, and look at us—
towering mountains of endless
dark matter, friends
only in name.*

Think of the darkest, deepest hell, 25
or what's beyond the farthest walls
of the world, where the sun never rises,
or what's under the earth,
or even on top of it at night,
during the rains. Now take all that thick
dense darkness and mix it together.
What you get will pale
before the blackness in my heart.

«sarv'|ânartha|prathama|karaṇe,
sarva|bhāvair jihāsye
dehe moho yadi pariṇataḥ,
poṣaṇīyo may"» êti
āstām evaṃ. «vapur idam iv' ā-
gāmi c' âsmākam ev',» êty
eṣ" âpy āstāṃ matir. iti paraṃ
dharma|śāstreṣu ghoṣaḥ.

kāmī kāma|vraṇa|parigataḥ
kāminīr eva hitvā
bhuṅkte paścād apagata|bhayaṃ
kāminīnāṃ sahasram.
itthaṃ|kāraṃ viṣaya|sukha|bhog'|
âikatānair narair apy
asmin dehe katipaya|dināny
eṣa bhogo vivarjyaḥ?

nyāyyād arthād api kim adhikaṃ
labhyam unmārga|vṛttyā?
vaidhād annād api kim adhikaṃ
paryudasteṣu bhojyam?
bhāryā|bhogād api bhavati kaḥ
paṇya|kāntāsu bhogaḥ?
prāyo «n'!» êti śruti|viṣayatā
viśva|mādhurya|hetuḥ.

So what if some people swear
by the body, the prime source
of all disasters, the one thing
that's always in the way? So what
if they believe that a brand new body,
just like this one, will be waiting?
Let them be. It sounds like dharma
to me.

Sometimes even the greatest lover
gets sick of love and sends away
his lovers (which doesn't stop him
from sleeping with thousands
when his appetite recovers).
But those who are truly driven
by the body's pleasure—couldn't they take
a few days' break?

Does money that you steal
buy you more?
Does forbidden food
really taste better
than what the scriptures allow?
Is sex with a whore
any different from sex
at home with your wife?
What makes anything truly sweet
is that one word:
"Don't!"

āstikyaṃ ced, dhanam akhilam apy
arthisāt kartum arhaṃ.
nāstikyaṃ cet, tad api sutarāṃ
bhoga|hetor apāsyam.
a|spṛṣṭv" âpi svayam ati|rahaḥ
sthāpyate yat tad antas,
tasmin hetuḥ ka? iti nibhṛtaṃ
tarkayāmo, na vidmaḥ.

śvānaḥ pucch'|âñcala|kuṭilatāṃ,
sūkarāḥ kukṣi|poṣaṃ,
kīśā danta|prakaṭana|vidhiṃ,
gardabhā rūkṣa|ghoṣam,
martyā vakṣaḥ|śvayathum api ca
strīṣu dṛṣṭvā ramante.
tat saundaryaṃ kim iti phalitaṃ,
tat tad a|jñānato 'nyat.

rantuṃ prāpto daśati daśanair
ānanaṃ cet priyāyā,
bhoktuṃ prāptaḥ kim iti na daśed
agra|hastaṃ pradātuḥ?
itthaṃ vyakte hṛdaya|januṣaḥ

If you believe in God,
you ought to give away all you have
to those who come begging.
If you believe in nothing,
spending money is even easier
and more fun, too.
But to stash it away
in some secret place
without even touching it?
There are some things
we'll never understand.

For dogs it's the curl
at the end of the tail.
For pigs, the ample belly.
For apes it's something in the way
they show their teeth.
For donkeys, that horrible
hee-haw. What turns men on
is a certain bulge
on a woman's chest.
That's the thing about beauty:
it's all illusion, and to each
his own.

If a man making love
bites the lips of his lover,
why won't he bite the hand
that feeds him? It's clear
as daylight: passion drives you
out of your mind. But is anyone ready

pāmar'|ônmādakatve
hātuṃ sadyaḥ prabhavati na ko 'py
antato lajjituṃ vā.

dārāḥ, putrāḥ, śayanam, aśanaṃ,
bhūṣan'|ācchādane vā,
yac c' ēdṛkṣaṃ pum|abhilaṣitaṃ—
teṣu mā|śabdikaḥ kaḥ?
kiṃ tv eteṣāṃ bhavati niyamaḥ
sevane ko 'pi ko 'pi.
dveṣas tasminn api yadi bhavet,
tatra vaktā Kṛtāntaḥ.

ved'|âbhyāsa|vyasana|rasikaiḥ
sthīyate—tāvatā kiṃ?
sūkṣmā buddhiḥ śrutam iva viśaty
a|śrutaṃ—tāvatā kim?
jalp'|ārambhe jayati niyataṃ
vādinas—tāvatā kiṃ?
nirved'|ārtaṃ na yadi hṛdayaṃ
śāntim abhyeti puṃsaḥ.

yas tv atyanta|vyavasita|matiḥ
saṃjighṛkṣeta dharmaṃ,
Khaṭvāṅg'|āder iva, na kim alaṃ

to call it quits? Or at least
to feel some shame?

Women, children, a soft bed
and a good meal, gadgets
and fancy clothes, everything
a man wants—nobody's saying
no, you can't have them.
It's just that there are,
how to put it, a few minor
restrictions. You find this annoying?
You'll just have to work it out
with Death in person.

So there are experts in the Veda
who recite with perfect pitch—
so what?
So there are sharp minds
that can crack a text at first sight—
so what?
So there are those who trounce their opponents
in the first round of debate—
so what?
What good is any of it if a man
is sick at heart and finds
no peace?

Some peoples' minds are super sharp.
If they want to fathom the whole of dharma,
half an hour should suffice.
(Think of King Khatvánga).*

tasya yām'|ârdham āyuḥ?
duṣ|pāṇḍityād apahṛta|matir
yaḥ punaḥ saṃśay'|ātmā,
kasmai tasya prabhavatu vṛthā
kākavad dīrgham āyuḥ?

35 arthā na syur yadi, vijahimo
dharmam arth'|âika|sādhyaṃ.
kāya|kleśaiḥ kati|kati|vidhaḥ
sādhanīyo na dharmaḥ?
kāyaḥ śrānto yadi bhavati, kas
tāvatā dharma|lopaś?
cittaṃ dattvā sakṛd api Śive
cintitaṃ sādhayāmaḥ.

sven' âiv' ôktaṃ Nigama|vacasā
bodhanīyās tu jīvā.
«jīvair ev',» êty api ca munibhiḥ
kāritaṃ dharma|śāstram.
«utpaśyantu svayam,» iti bhavo
dāruṇaś cālyate 'sāv.
ady' âpi smo yadi khalu jaḍāḥ,
kiṃ vidhattāṃ Śivo 'pi?

yen' ācāntāḥ salila|nidhayo,
yena sṛṣṭā pratidyauḥ,
śāstrāṇy astrāṇy api kabalitāny

Then there are those whose minds are ruined
by too much learning, and whose hearts
are filled with doubt. No matter how long
they may live, even as long as a crow,
it's a total waste
of time.

If you're out of money, go for the pieties
that money just can't buy.
After all, there are so many ways
to torture your body for a good cause.
And once the body's worn out, don't worry.
So you'll end up with a little less religion
to your credit. But turn your thoughts just once
to God, and all you wished for
is true.

First he tried to teach us in his own words
and came up with the Veda.
Then he thought people might want to learn
from people like themselves, so he had the sages
write the law books. Then he wanted us to see it
for ourselves, so he made life into this horrible
race to death. If we haven't got it
by now, there's no more
God can do.

One drank up entire oceans.
Another created a parallel world
in the skies. A third, with one hand,
held up a staff that devoured

ekayā yasya yaṣṭyā,
kas tādṛkṣaḥ prabhavatu jano
deva|bhūdeva varge?
kālaḥ kīṭān iva kabalayām
āsa tān apy a|yatnam.

kāya|sthairyaṃ, karaṇa|paṭutāṃ,
bandhu|saṃpattim, arthaṃ,
cāturyaṃ vā—kim iva hi balaṃ
bibhrato nirbharāḥ smaḥ.
antyaḥ śvāsaḥ kim ayam atha v" ôp-
āntya, ity āmṛśanto
vismṛty' Ēśaṃ nimiṣam api kiṃ
vartituṃ pārayāmaḥ?

«abhyasy' ādau śrutim, atha gṛhaṃ
prāpya, labdhvā mah"|ârthān,
iṣṭvā yajñair, janita|tanayaḥ
pravrajed āyuṣo 'nte.»
ity ācaṣṭe ya iha sa Manur
Yājñavalkyo 'pi vā me,

any weapon hurled against it.
They don't make them like that
anymore, not as gods, not as men.
And even they fell prey to Time,
who casually gobbled them up
like worms.*

A body that's still in one piece,
senses in good working order,
friends and family,
a steady flow of cash,
a savvy mind,
and sheer physical strength—
so long as we bear this burden,
we're light at heart. But if we reach the point
of wondering if this is our last breath,
or maybe one before the last,
how can we go on
for even one more second
not thinking
of God?

"First, study the Veda.
Then build a home.
Make money.
Perform the rituals.
Father children.
Then, at the end of your life,
set out for the forest."
Sounds good. I'm all for it, if only
Manu, or Yajna·valkya, or whoever said it,

tāvat kālaṃ pratibhavati ced
āyuṣas tat pramāṇam.

annaṃ, dhānyaṃ, vasu, vasumat' îty
uttaren' ôttareṇa
vyākṛṣyante parama|kṛpaṇāḥ
pāmarā yadvad ittham,
bhūmiḥ, khaṃ, dyaur, Druhiṇa|gṛham ity
uttareṇ' ôttareṇa
vyāmuhyante vimala|matayo 'py
a|sthireṇ' âiva dhāmnā.

prāyaś|cittaṃ sakṛd|upanate
vā pramādāt kṛte vā.
bhūyo bhūyo 'py avahitataraiḥ
sādhite kaḥ samādhiḥ?
kāruṇy'|âbdhir yadi Puraharaḥ,
satsu kāmaṃ dayeta.
bhraṣṭe mādṛśy api sa dayate
cet, kṣato dharma|setuḥ.

sādhyā Śambhoḥ katham api day" êty
apy a|sādhy'|ôpadeśaḥ.
kopaṃ tasya prathamam apanudy'
âiva sādhyaḥ prasādaḥ.
kopo varṇ'|āśrama|niyamit'|ā-
cāra|nirlaṅghan'|ôtthaḥ

can guarantee exactly how long
I have to live.

Food, crops, hard cash, real estate—
that's what people want, more and more,
pathetic fools that they are.
This world, the one above it, the one above that,
Brahma's heaven—even pious minds
are fooled, more and more,
into thinking they'll stay there
forever.

A single glitch,
a moment's inattention—
there are ways to make amends.
But if you commit the crime
over and over, well aware,
there's no repair. Let's say that Shiva,
Burner of Cities, is an ocean
of mercy. Let's say he pardons
the pious. The dam of dharma
will burst if he pardons
a swindler like me.

They say that somehow,
by hook or by crook,
we can win God's compassion.
Yet another pointless sermon.
To win his gracious attention
we would first have to cool his anger.
But it's not for nothing that he's angry—

śāntiṃ neyaḥ sa katham adhun" âpy
a|vyavasthā|pravṛttaiḥ?

iṣṭ'|āpūrtair, nigama|paṭhanaiḥ,
kṛcchra|cāndrāyaṇ'|ādyaiḥ,
svāminn, anyair api tava manaḥ
kāmam āvarjayema,
madhye madhye yadi na nipatet
karmaṇā coditānāṃ
jñānaṃ śraddh" êty ubhayam api no
jāti|vairy|argal" êva.

nir|maryādaḥ, parama|capalo,
niḥ|samājñāna|rāśir
mādṛkṣo 'nyaḥ ka iti bhuvane
mārgaṇīyaṃ tvay" âiva?
«īdṛkṣe 'pi kva|cid iha dayey',»
êti kautūhalaṃ cet,
svāmin Viśveśvara, tava, bhavaṃ
nistareyaṃ tad" âham.

we keep breaking all his rules.
So how do you expect him to cool off
when even now, at this very minute,
we can't keep out of trouble?

Rituals, good deeds, recitation
of the Vedas, a whole month of fasting—
it seems, Lord, that with all of these
we might just be able to open
your heart, if only Trust
and Awareness, the two treacherous
keys, don't desert us
in the act.

Unruly,
utterly reckless,
an ocean of mindlessness—
just see if you can find,
anywhere in this world, someone
like me. And if, God of Everything,
you happen to wonder
if you're capable of feeling
for some such creature,
then even I,
Lord,
stand a chance
of reaching the shore.

paścāt|taptāḥ katham api vidheḥ
kiṃkarī|bhūya kurmaḥ
sevāṃ Śambhor, iti ca niyamaṃ
v" âpi saṃkalpayāmaḥ.
āyuḥ kiṃ me? kim iva karaṇaṃ?
dus|tare saṃkaṭe 'smin,
svāmin Gaurī|ramaṇa, śaraṇaṃ
nas tvam eva, tvam eva.

samyaṅ|muktās tribhir api malaiś,
cid|vikās'|âika|rūpās,
tvan|nidhyāna|pravaṇa|manasaḥ
sūrayas tvat|pure ye,
teṣāṃ saṃdarśayitum a|pari-
jñāta|pūrvaṃ kadā cij
jantuṃ mugdhaṃ, Śiva, nayasi kiṃ
viśva|pāraṃ puraṃ mām?

Suppose I somehow bring myself 45
to slave away at dharma and to serve
God. Suppose I even regret all I did
and swear not to swerve
from duty. How much life
do I have left?
What means can I muster?
In these dire straits,
Lord,
Gauri's Lover,
my only hope is
you
you
you.

Your heaven is packed with pure souls.
They're totally free from the three stains.*
Their minds flow into you.
They're awareness itself
remade into light.
Wouldn't you like to show them, just once,
something new, something they've never ever seen,
a truly stupid creature?
That way you can take me
to your city
beyond this world.

diṣṭyā labdhaṃ dvija|vara|kule
janma. tatr' âpi diṣṭyā
dharm'|â|dharma|sthitir avagat" âi-
va prasādād gurūṇām.
janmany asminn api yadi na me
saṃbhaved āstikatvaṃ,
nistāraḥ kiṃ niraya|bhavanāt
sarva|mokṣe 'pi labhyaḥ?

bhavye dehe, paṭuṣu karaṇeṣv,
ālaye śrī|samṛddhe,
kaumār'|ânte vayasi, katham apy
a|pravṛtte ca duḥkhe
pratyak|puṣpī|prasava|vidhayā
yasya puṃso nisargāt
pratyag|vaktraṃ bhavati hṛdayaṃ,
kas tato 'py asti dhanyaḥ?

n' âhaṃ yāce padam uḍu|pater,
n' âdhikāraṃ Maghono,
n' âpi Brāhmīṃ bhavana|gurutāṃ.
kā kath" ânya|prapañce?
anyasy' ânyaḥ śriyam abhilaṣann

So I was lucky.
I was born into the best Brahmin family.
And lucky again—
all those lectures on ethics,
on what's good and what's bad,
from the finest professors.
If after all this, in this best
of all possible lives,
I still can't bring myself
to believe, how will I ever
be free? Even if everyone else
is released, I'll still be stuck here,
in hell.

Let's say you have a healthy body,
acute senses, a well-appointed house.
Let's say you're still young and,
somehow or other, suffering
hasn't yet begun. And then,
if your heart turns inward
of its own accord, like a flower
that curves back on its stem,
I'd be prepared to call you
a lucky man.

I'm not asking for the moon,
Indra's throne, or Brahma's heaven,
let alone some other galaxy.
What place is left for you if you want to be
someone else? All I'm asking for,
Shiva,

astu kas tasya loko?
mahyaṃ, Śambho, diśa masṛṇitaṃ
māmak'|ānandam eva.

ā garbhād, ā kula|parivṛḍād,
ā Caturvaktrato 'pi
tvat|pād'|âbja|prapadana|parān
vetsi naś, Candramaule.
māyāyāś ca prapadana|pareṣv
a|pravṛttiṃ tvam āttha.
svāminn, evaṃ sati yad ucitaṃ,
tatra devaḥ pramāṇam.

daṇḍaṃ dhatte sakala|jagatāṃ
dakṣiṇo yaḥ Kṛtānto,
nām' âpy asya pratibhaya|tanor
n' ôpagṛhṇīmah' îti.
prāptāḥ smas taṃ, Nigama|vacasām
uttaro yaḥ Kṛtānto.
yad vā tad vā bhavatu. na punas
tasya paśyema vaktram.

iti śrī Nīlakaṇṭhadīkṣita|viracitaḥ Śāntivilāsaḥ saṃpūrṇaḥ.

is that gentle feeling
that is mine.

You know very well,
Moon-crested God,
that we're already at your feet
from the moment we are born,
from the very beginning
of this family, going back
to Brahma himself.
You've also said that the world
has no hold over anyone
who throws himself at your feet.
That's where things stand,
Lord.
From here on,
it's up to you.

Death who?
If you mean the End of Everything,
that scary guy who lives in the south
and carries a staff—we can't even remember
his name. If he turns up,
we won't give him a second look.
If you mean the End of the Vedas,
the one who's far beyond, way up north—
we stick to him. Whatever will be,
let it be.

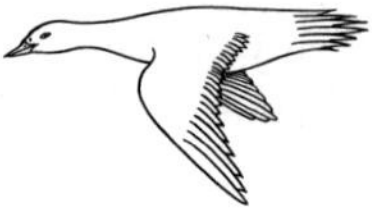

NOTES

Bold *references are to the English text;* ***bold italic*** *references are to the Sanskrit text. An asterisk (*) in the body of the text marks the word or passage being annotated.*

The Mission of the Goose

1.1 Rama's lineage, the *sūrya/vaṃśa*, traces itself back to the sun. The family is also known as the Ikshvákus (e.g. 1.8). Sita is the daughter of Jánaka, king of Míthila.

1.6 The ultimate godhead is often pictured as a goose that lives in both worlds—the heavens and the water on earth. Geese are believed to be able to extract milk from a mixture of milk and water. Perhaps, by extension, the Brahma-goose could make sense of the oceanic Veda. Both Brahma, the creator, and Sarásvati, his wife and goddess of speech, ride a goose.

1.7 **Brahma ... worked for Shiva**: when Shiva fought the demons of the Triple City, Brahma served as his charioteer.

1.10 Sanskrit **peacocks** screech and dance in ecstasy as soon as they catch sight of the monsoon clouds. The autumn, however, is the season of Sanskrit geese. This verse seemingly repeats this convention in celebrating the relief one gets when the rains subside and the peacocks stop their annoying clamor. In addition, there is a pun (*śleṣa*) in this verse: *sat/kavi* means both a good bird and a true poet, hence the translation **noble songbird**. In the absence of such a poet-bird, the *vipina/śikhinaḥ*, both peacocks and boorish brahmins, have a field day, chattering idiocies that deafen the ears. They only quiet down when the clouds retreat and the true poet-bird is back. The poet repeats the pun on *kavi* (bird/poet) elsewhere in the poem: 1.29, 1.47.

1.12 The name of the red **bandhu·jiva flower** alludes to supporting the life of a friend. Párvati, wife of god Shiva, is the daughter of Mount

Himálaya. Shiva's other wife, the Ganges, flows from heaven to earth through his hair.

1.14 Sita was discovered by her father, king Jánaka, in a furrow he was plowing. Hence her name, which means "furrow."

1.16 **Savage beauties**: women of the Shábari tribe.

1.18 The road not taken goes through the **Sahya Hills**, which form the Western Ghats.

1.21–24 Verses 21–24 describe Tirupati, today a major pilgrimage center on the Andhra-Tamil border. The mountain ridge on which the temple is situated is sometimes named Sheshádri, as the mountain is believed to be identical with the primordial snake Shesha, on whom Vishnu rests. Another name for it is Mount Ánjana. This mountain also hosts Compassion, the goddess praised in Vedánta Déshika's other poem in this volume. Snakes are believed to have precious stones in the middle of their hoods.

1.23 The river **Rushing Gold** is usually known as Suvárna·múkhari, and the Shiva temple on its bank is the famous Kala·hasti, home to the *liṅga* of wind.

1.25 The northern Tamil coastal plain is known as Tondai·nadu, **Tundíra** in Sanskrit. Its major pilgrimage city is Kanchi·puram (Kanchi). Local tradition has it that Sarásvati, enraged at her husband Brahma for performing a ritual with another of his wives (Savítri), turned into a gushing river, Végavati, in order to ruin the rite. Vishnu came to Brahma's rescue as a *setu*, or **dyke**, blocking her way.

1.26 **Kanchi** (Kāñcī) literally means a belt or a cincture. **Elephant Hill** (Hastigiri or Hastiśaila) is the site of the Várada·raja·svami Temple. Púrusha, the primordial person, is one of Vishnu's names.

1.29 **Seven sets of sounds**: velar stops, palatals, retroflexes, dentals, labials, nasals and sibilants, as defined by Indian phonologists. **Sarásvati** is also worshipped as a river.

1.33 The cloud in question, at least on one level, is the dark icon of Várada·raja·svami/Vishnu in Kanchi·puram. On the breast of this image we find Lakshmi, who is thus appropriately likened to a flash of lightning within the dark monsoon cloud. At the feet of this emerald-colored Vishnu lie the most accomplished devotees, the *nitya/sūris*, who have been granted the honorific title of *deva/haṃsa*, heavenly geese (*haṃsa* or *parama/haṃsa* are common titles for advanced ascetics or seers). What is more, the Cloud-cum-god has become yet another goose in the sense that he is identical to the supreme reality, referred to already in the Upaniṣads by the same word, *haṃsa*. As such, he must be the First Goose, and hence the founder of the entire species of which our messenger is the latest representative.

1.38 The **White Cliff** (*Śvetādri*) is the temple at Tiru·vallarai, close to Śrīraṅgam (according to N. V. Desika Chariar and Kasturi Ranga Ayengar).

1.39 **Ocean's daughter** is Lakshmi, who was born from the ocean of milk.

1.40 V.l. : *nīlī/puṣpa/stabakalalitam* for ***nīlīrakṣā/niyata/lalitam*** in *pāda* b. Most commentators prefer the latter reading and regard the former as a modern interpolation.

1.40 **Indigo** (Nili) is the fiercest of Tamil folk goddesses; the *māhātmya* texts from Śrīraṅgam refer to her role as the guardian of the *Nīlī/vanam*, the forest described in this verse. This description of the Nili forest inaugurates a series of verses dealing with the famous shrine in Śrīraṅgam (1.40–46).

1.42 Sanskrit **pearls** emerge from the joints of the sugar cane, among other sources.

1.43 **High-born birds**: the Sanskrit word *dvija* refers to all who have two births, including brahmins (born a second time at their ritual initiation) and birds (born as an egg and from an egg).

1.44 **Lake Mánasa** in Tibet is the nesting place of Indian geese, who spend the rainy season there.

1.45 Today, as in the poet's time, the Shri·ranga·vimána houses the central image of the god at Śrīraṅgam. After having been kept for years in Ayódhya, it was given by Rama to Vibhíshana as a gift in return for his help and loyalty in the Lanka war. Vibhíshana tried to take it south to Lanka, but on the way he parked it in Śrīraṅgam, in order to celebrate a festival with the Chola king. When he tried to pick it up again, he could not move it; the god appeared and informed him that the *vimāna* would remain permanently at Śrīraṅgam as a result of *tapas* performed by the Kavéri river, and that he himself intended to stay there too. However, all of this, from the point of view of Rama and the goose, is still far in the future. As he addresses the goose, the Shesha throne, on which the *vimāna* will later come to rest, stands empty beside the Moon Pond.

1.47 The dry **wild region** south of the Kavéri delta is associated with Kallar hunters, from the period of Tamil *caṅkam* poetry onward.

1.49 The site is Alagar·malai or Vrishabhádri, near Madurai, where the god is Alagar ("beautiful," Sanskrit *Sundarabāhu*). When Vishnu as Tri·víkrama stretched his foot to the end of the cosmos, the stream known as the Núpura·ganga ("The Ganges of the Anklet") flowed directly from his anklet to this mountain. This version of the Ganges's appearance on earth intentionally does away with Shiva's role in blocking its water with his hair.

1.50 According to the Madurai tradition, a Pandya king once imprisoned the rain-**clouds** for failing to water their fields. Álaka, the home of Kubéra lord of the *yakṣas*, is the goal of Kali·dasa's cloud-messenger.

1.51 In the far south of the Tamil country, we find the Tamra·parni river, famous for its pearly oysters, and Mount Podiyil, where the Vedic dwarf-sage Agástya resides. Agástya once drank up the entire ocean in order to expose the Kaléya demons, enemies of the gods, hidden in its water. Agástya is also the star Canopus, which rises in the autumn when the rain-soaked land dries out. See Hiltebeitel (1977).

1.56 **The steed that Indra stole**: King Ságara, one of Rama's ancestors, performed 99 horse-sacrifices. Had he completed the hundredth he would have inherited the throne of Indra, king of the gods; so Indra stole the hundredth horse and hid it under the earth. Ságara's 60,000 sons searched for the horse by digging up the earth. They found it only to be burnt up by the sage Kápila, who was keeping an eye on it. Ságara's great grandson, Bhagi·ratha, wanted to purify their ashes and succeeded in bringing the Ganges all the way from heaven to that hole, which then became the ocean. **Submarine mountains ... whose wings are still intact**: on a different occasion, at the time when mountains still had wings, Indra went to war against them, and managed to maim and immobilize them. A few survivors, such as Mount Mainaka, flew to find refuge in the southern seas. When Hánuman leapt over the ocean to Lanka—thus preceding our goose on this route—Mainaka rose up and offered him a resting place. Note the multiple reciprocities the poet has built into the two halves of this verse: the ocean returns a favor to Rama's lineage, the sea and the earth enter one another, and Indra is the violent catalyst of both the mountains' taking refuge in the ocean and the ocean's expansion to envelop the earth.

1.58 In the beginning, mountains had wings and could fly. Indra cut off their wings in order to fix them in place. See note to 1.56.

2.1 **Heart Lake**: Lake Mánasa in Tibet.

2.5 **Vishva·karman** is the architect and builder of the gods, who built Lanka for Rávana.

2.9 Rama **won** Sita by bending and breaking Shiva's great bow in the palace of her father, Jánaka.

2.17 Soon after Rama and Sita entered the forest they were hosted by sage Atri and his **wife Anasúya**, who gave Sita aromatherapy.

2.20 At the time Rávana kidnapped Sita and carried her through the air to Lanka, she cast **down to earth** some of her ornaments and clothes, in the hope that Rama would find them and follow her.

2.28 **Autumn**, when the rains have dried up and the geese return from the north, is the preferred season for military campaigns.

2.33 The sense seems to be that the night goes on and on because it is fragmented to series of endless and unbearable fantasies and anxieties. The other reading conceives of the night as a relentless, undifferentiated sequence of time.

2.37 As Rama remembers his wedding with Sita his thoughts turn guiltily to his father-in-law, **Jánaka**.

2.42 V.l. *dūre kartur* for ***dūre kṛtvā*** in *pāda* d, according to which Rama himself has driven Sita away.

2.47 If you don't happen to know the **Nala** story, here is a clue. The famous lovers Nala and Damayánti first connect with one another through the agency of a talking goose. See "Maha·bhárata" 3.50.

Compassion

4 **Paráshara** is the father of Vyasa, the compiler of the Vedas.

4 **The man who brought the Ganges down to earth** is Bhagi·ratha. See note to "Mission of the Goose," 1.56.

7 **Bull Hill** is Vrisha·giri, or Vénkatam, the mountain at Tirupati.

8 **Nila**: Vishnu's third consort.

10 **Ánjana Hill**: Another name for Venkatádri.

16 **Your dance**: *pratisañcara/keli*, literally the "play of the exit"—a term for the *pralaya* flood that destroys the cosmos at the end of every cycle and for the retreat to backstage of the actress or dancer.

21 The image is of dry fields flooded at the end of the hot season so that rice can begin to sprout.

22 The verse is built around the famous story of the churning of the **ocean of milk** by the gods and demons, using Mount Mándara as the churning rod. The point of the exercise was to produce *amṛta*, the elixir of immortality, which was then stored in the moon.

31 Vishnu is the slayer of the demon **Madhu** and his ally Káitabha.

37 **Remind them of each other**: the commentators differ on the question of who has to be reminded of whom. Is it God, the direct object of *smarayasi* who is so preoccupied with his games that Compassion has to remind him of his dying neighbors, or is it they who need to be helped to make God their final, liberating thought (*antima/smṛti*). We feel that a close reading of the verse suggests that both parties could use a reminder.

39 **Precious souls**: these include the *nitya* (*sūris*) and the *mukta*, or liberated, with a pun on *muktā*—pearl.

45 **Lion Hill**: yet another name for Venkatáchala.

48 *Udghāta* refers here to the syllable "*oṃ*" that opens up and encapsulates the Vedic mantras.

50 **Kshatra·bandhu** was a bandit, with many murders to his credit, when a sage happened to cross his path and tried to reform him. Kshatra·bandhu declared it was too late for him to change his lifestyle. So the sage recommended that he cry "Govínda!"—the name of god—every time he coughed or sneezed. This was enough to redeem this criminal.

54 **Three great boons**: according to the commentators: mastery, autonomy and final freedom (*aiśvarya*, *kaivalya*, *mokṣa*).

61 **Burning under the waves**: a fire, burning in the form of a mare's head (*vaḍav'/ânala*), exists deep in the ocean, and feeds off its water until, at doomsday, it bursts out to burn the world.

64 This verse alludes to three episodes from the "Ramáyana." Rama threatened the ocean at the time he needed to cross it en route to Lanka. The ocean submitted and asked him to shoot his arrow at his (the ocean's) enemies ("Ramáyana" 6.22). Párashu·rama, an earlier avatar of Vishnu, came to fight Rama after the latter had broken Shiva's bow to win Sita. Rama overcame him and his somewhat pedantic objections. When a crow pecked at Sita's breast while Rama was sleeping on her lap in the forest, Rama released his arrow at him. The crow begged forgiveness, so Rama, instead of killing him, left him with one eye, which oscillates between the two sockets. The verse leads up to a powerful oxymoron: Vishnu is *vilīna/svātantrya*. Literally, his independence is dependent on your game.

65 Guha, the **chief of the hunters** on the banks of the Ganges, took Rama and his party across the river on their way into exile—and became Rama's close friend. Sugríva, a somewhat unsavory **king of the monkeys**, became Rama's most important ally. The **tribal** Shábari fed Rama and Sita a sweet meal of nuts and berries in the wilderness. Kuchéla was a **pauper** who came to Krishna's house carrying a gift of a few grains of parched rice, and returned home to find himself a rich man. The **hunchback** Kubja was embraced and straightened up by Krishna on the road. The **cowgirls** of Braj were the lovers of the adolescent Krishna.

71 **Conscious beings** are divided into *baddhas*, *muktas* and *nityas*. **Unconscious beings** are divided into *prakṛti*, *kāla*, and *śuddha/sattva*.

73 **Oldest emanations**: *vyūha*—Vasudéva, Sankárshana, Pradyúmna, Anirúddha—a sequence of four Vaishnava emanations, known from early iconography and the *āgamas*.

75 **Self-possession**: the modern commentators identify *ātm'|ânubhūti* with *kaivalya*: self-isolation or autonomy that is associated with release.

83 Bhu·devi, or Earth, was stolen and hidden at the bottom of the sea by the demon Hiranyáksha. Vishnu took the form of the wild boar, Varáha, killed the demon, and lifted up the earth on his tusk.

84 When the demon king Hiránya·káshipu denied the omnipresence of Vishnu and dared his son, Prahláda, to make this god emerge from a pillar, Vishnu burst out of that pillar in the form of a raging man-lion and disemboweled the demon.

85 The allusion is to the Vámana avatar, in which Vishnu, the dwarf, expanded to the limit of the cosmos, which he covered with three steps.

86 Both editions have *paraśvatha* at the beginning of *a*, for the dictionary's *paraśvadha*.

86 Párashu·rama wiped out the kings of this earth twenty-one times and sacrificed their blood to the ancestors. According to our poet, the dying kings, like sacrificial animals, reached heaven through the mindful intervention of Daya.

87 Rama built the bridge with the help of the monkeys to cross the ocean to Rávana's island, Lanka.

88 **Bala·rama** is Krishna's older brother: brawny, unreflective, and with a fondness for wine.

89 **That Song**: the "Bhagavad Gita," sung by Krishna at the time of the "Maha·bhárata" war.

90 Kalkin, the future avatar of Vishnu, comes as a warrior on horseback to destroy evildoers at the end of time and to allow the first golden eon in the cycle of time to start again.

95 Here is what a modern south Indian commentator has to say about this remarkable verse: "I went to hide, far away. You mustn't take

this quietly. You have to find me, lift me up, and possess me. Your husband [Vishnu] lives on this mountain—and like any king, he likes to hunt. Take advantage of this excuse. You should turn into a trap, a long one, and catch me. I will try to escape like any wild animal, biting and clawing my way out, but you must pin me down and deliver me to your husband. Though I try to escape, you will be a trap so large and well-constructed that I won't be able to break free." (Nallūr Śrīnivāsa Rāghavācārya Svāmi).

101 The Tamil commentator Nallūr Śrīnivāsa Rāghavācārya Svāmi notes that God's powers constitute the first audience for the *Dayā-śataka* and offer the first confirmation of this great work.

Self-Surrender

7 **Burner of Passion**: *Smara*, literally "memory," is one of the names of the god of desire, or passion, burnt to ashes by Shiva.

13 **When all systems fail**, literally, tormented by all three bodily humors, or *doṣas* (bile, phlegm, and wind). According to Śivānanda Yati, however, the three *doṣas* are not humors but faults of spiritual, physical and divine origin.

22 V.l. *hastālambaprapadanam* for ***hastālambaprapatanam*** in *d*. If this alternative reading is correct, however, the poet's confidence in the outstretched hand is the result of his own act of surrender, or *prapadana* (= *prapatti*). Note that for a Tamil speaker the two options are homophonous.

23 **They cast their hopes on a welcoming smile from you**: *dakṣiṇaṃ mukham* is Shiva's gentle aspect, one of his three (or sometimes five) faces. *Dakṣiṇam* is also south, thus perhaps suggesting Shiva's accessibility to his southern devotees, particularly in his form as Marga·saháya, the friend to the traveler, in his temple in Virinji·puram, where he was worshiped by Appayya. This form of the god seems to be indicated by the opening of this verse.

48 Cf. *Kuvalayānanda* of Appayya Díkshita p. 73, ad. *nidarśaṇā*.

Peace

5 **Killer of Passion**: see note to “Self-Surrender,” 7.

9 **The journey must begin with a certain something**: journeys usually begin with a formal ritual to ensure their success, referred to here as *vidhi*, or prescribed rite.

24 **Friends only in name**: literally, *brahma/bandhu* is a pejorative epithet meaning “brahmin only by name.”

34 **Think of King Khatvánga**: this king was informed by the gods that he had less than an hour left to live; he quickly renounced all worldly desires and turned to Vishnu, who granted him release (*Bhāgavata Purāṇa* 2.1, 9.9).

37 The dwarf Agástya swallowed the ocean in order to expose the demons hiding in it. Vishva·mitra created an upside-down heaven for his protégé, King Tri·shanku. The **staff** of sage Vasíshtha easily devoured the arrows that his rival Vishva·mitra aimed at him.

46 **The three stains**: *āṇava*, *māyika*, and *kārmika*: stains which are congenital, inbuilt, and generated by one’s own actions.

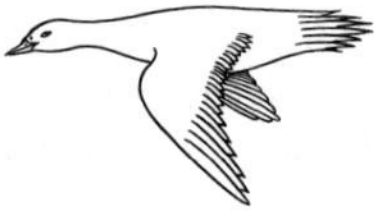

THE CLAY SANSKRIT LIBRARY

Current Volumes

For further details please consult the CSL website.

1. The Emperor of the Sorcerers (*Bṛhatkathāślokasaṃgraha*) (vol. 1 of 2) by *Budhasvāmin*. Sir James Mallinson
2. Heavenly Exploits (*Divyāvadāna*). Joel Tatelman
3. Maha·bhárata III: The Forest (*Vanaparvan*) (vol. 4 of 4) William J. Johnson
4. Much Ado about Religion (*Āgamaḍambara*) by *Bhaṭṭa Jayanta*. Csaba Dezső
5. The Birth of Kumára (*Kumārasaṃbhava*) by *Kālidāsa*. David Smith
6. Ramáyana I: Boyhood (*Bālakāṇḍa*) by *Vālmīki*. Robert P. Goldman
7. The Epitome of Queen Lilávati (*Līlāvatīsāra*) (vol. 1 of 2) by *Jinaratna*. R.C.C. Fynes
8. Ramáyana II: Ayódhya (*Ayodhyākāṇḍa*) by *Vālmīki*. Sheldon I. Pollock
9. Love Lyrics (*Amaruśataka, Śatakatraya & Caurapañcāśikā*) by *Amaru, Bhartṛhari & Bilhaṇa*. Greg Bailey & Richard Gombrich
10. What Ten Young Men Did (*Daśakumāracarita*) by *Daṇḍin*. Isabelle Onians
11. Three Satires (*Kaliviḍambana, Kalāvilāsa & Bhallaṭaśataka*) by *Nīlakaṇṭha, Kṣemendra & Bhallaṭa*. Somadeva Vasudeva
12. Ramáyana IV: Kishkíndha (*Kiṣkindhākāṇḍa*) by *Vālmīki*. Rosalind Lefeber
13. The Emperor of the Sorcerers (*Bṛhatkathāślokasaṃgraha*) (vol. 2 of 2) by *Budhasvāmin*. Sir James Mallinson
14. Maha·bhárata IX: Shalya (*Śalyaparvan*) (vol. 1 of 2) Justin Meiland
15. Rákshasa's Ring (*Mudrārākṣasa*) by *Viśākhadatta*. Michael Coulson

16. Messenger Poems (*Meghadūta, Pavanadūta & Haṃsadūta*) by *Kālidāsa, Dhoyī & Rūpa Gosvāmin.* Sir James Mallinson
17. Ramáyana III: The Forest (*Araṇyakāṇḍa*) by *Vālmīki.* Sheldon I. Pollock
18. The Epitome of Queen Lilávati (*Līlāvatīsāra*) (vol. 2 of 2) by *Jinaratna.* R.C.C. Fynes
19. Five Discourses on Worldly Wisdom (*Pañcatantra*) by *Viṣṇuśarman.* Patrick Olivelle
20. Ramáyana V: Súndara (*Sundarakāṇḍa*) by *Vālmīki.* Robert P. Goldman & Sally J. Sutherland Goldman
21. Maha·bhárata II: The Great Hall (*Sabhāparvan*) Paul Wilmot
22. The Recognition of Shakúntala (*Abhijñānaśākuntala*) (Kashmir Recension) by *Kālidāsa.* Somadeva Vasudeva
23. Maha·bhárata VII: Drona (*Droṇaparvan*) (vol. 1 of 4) Vaughan Pilikian
24. Rama Beyond Price (*Anargharāghava*) by *Murāri.* Judit Törzsök
25. Maha·bhárata IV: Viráta (*Virāṭaparvan*) Kathleen Garbutt
26. Maha·bhárata VIII: Karna (*Karṇaparvan*) (vol. 1 of 2) Adam Bowles
27. "The Lady of the Jewel Necklace" & "The Lady who Shows her Love" (*Ratnāvalī & Priyadarśikā*) by *Harṣa.* Wendy Doniger
28. The Ocean of the Rivers of Story (*Kathāsaritsāgara*) (vol. 1 of 7) by *Somadeva.* Sir James Mallinson
29. Handsome Nanda (*Saundarananda*) by *Aśvaghoṣa.* Linda Covill
30. Maha·bhárata IX: Shalya (*Śalyaparvan*) (vol. 2 of 2) Justin Meiland
31. Rama's Last Act (*Uttararāmacarita*) by *Bhavabhūti.* Sheldon Pollock. Foreword by Girish Karnad
32. "Friendly Advice" (*Hitopadeśa*) by *Nārāyaṇa* & "King Víkrama's Adventures" (*Vikramacarita*). Judit Törzsök

33. Life of the Buddha (*Buddhacarita*)
by *Aśvaghoṣa*. Patrick Olivelle
34. Maha·bhárata V: Preparations for War (*Udyogaparvan*)
(vol. 1 of 2). Kathleen Garbutt.
Foreword by Gurcharan Das
35. Maha·bhárata VIII: Karna (*Karṇaparvan*) (vol. 2 of 2)
Adam Bowles
36. Maha·bhárata V: Preparations for War (*Udyogaparvan*)
(vol. 2 of 2). Kathleen Garbutt
37. Maha·bhárata VI: Bhishma (*Bhīṣmaparvan*) (vol. 1 of 2)
Including the "Bhagavad Gita" in Context
Alex Cherniak. Foreword by Ranajit Guha
38. The Ocean of the Rivers of Story (*Kathāsaritsāgara*) (vol. 2 of 7)
by *Somadeva*. Sir James Mallinson
39. "How the Nagas were Pleased" (*Nāgānanda*) by *Harṣa* &
"The Shattered Thighs" (*Ūrubhaṅga*) by *Bhāsa*.
Andrew Skilton
40. Gita·govínda: Love Songs of Radha and Krishna (*Gītagovinda*)
by *Jayadeva*. Lee Siegel. Foreword by Sudipta Kaviraj
41. "Bouquet of Rasa" & "River of Rasa" (*Rasamañjarī & Rasataraṅgiṇī*) by *Bhānudatta*. Sheldon Pollock
42. Garland of the Buddha's Past Lives (*Jātakamālā*) (vol. 1 of 2)
by *Āryaśūra*. Justin Meiland
43. Maha·bhárata XII: Peace (*Śāntiparvan*) (vol. 3 of 5)
"The Book of Liberation" (*Mokṣadharma*). Alexander Wynne
44. The Little Clay Cart (*Mṛcchakaṭikā*) by *Śūdraka*.
Diwakar Acharya. Foreword by Partha Chatterjee
45. Bhatti's Poem: The Death of Rávana (*Bhaṭṭikāvya*)
by *Bhaṭṭi*. Oliver Fallon
46. "Self-Surrender," "Peace," "Compassion," and "The Mission of the Goose": Poems and Prayers from South India
(*Ātmārpaṇastuti, Śāntivilāsa, Dayāśataka & Haṃsasaṃdeśa*)
by *Appayya Dīkṣita, Nīlakaṇṭha Dīkṣita & Vedānta Deśika.*
Yigal Bronner & David Shulman
Foreword by Gieve Patel

To Appear in 2009

Garland of the Buddha's Past Lives (*Jātakamālā*) (vol. 2 of 2) by *Āryaśūra*. JUSTIN MEILAND

How Úrvashi Was Won (*Vikramorvaśīya*) by *Kālidāsa* VELCHERU NARAYANA RAO & DAVID SHULMAN

Maha·bhárata VI: Bhishma (*Bhīṣmaparvan*) (vol. 2 of 2) ALEX CHERNIAK

Maha·bhárata VII: Drona (*Droṇaparvan*) (vol. 2 of 4) VAUGHAN PILIKIAN

Maha·bhárata X & XI: Dead of the Night & The Women (*Sauptikaparvan & Strīparvan*). KATE CROSBY

Málavika and Agni·mitra (*Mālavikāgnimitram*) by *Kālidāsa*. DÁNIEL BALOGH & ESZTER SOMOGYI

Princess Kadámbari (*Kādambarī*) (vol. 1 of 3) by *Bāṇa*. DAVID SMITH

The Quartet of Causeries (*Caturbhāṇī*) by *Śūdraka, Śyāmilaka, Vararuci & Īśvaradatta*. CSABA DEZSŐ & SOMADEVA VASUDEVA

The Rise of Wisdom Moon (*Prabodhacandrodaya*) by *Kṛṣṇamiśra*. MATTHEW KAPSTEIN

Seven Hundred Elegant Verses (*Āryāsaptaśatī*) by *Govardhana*. FRIEDHELM HARDY